Mysteries Of The Deep Blue

Mysteries Of The Deep Blue

Maria .M

Noble Publishing

CONTENTS

	INDEX	1
1	Introduction	3
2	Chapter 1	8
3	Chapter 2	29
4	Chapter 3	50
5	Chapter 4	75
6	Chapter 5	98
7	Chapter 6	121
8	Chapter 7	147
9	Conclusion	172

INDEX

Introduction

Chapter 1: "The Enigmatic Depths"
1.1 Introduction to the mysterious world beneath the ocean's surface.
1.2 Historical overview of human fascination with the deep sea.
1.3 Brief exploration of uncharted territories and the challenges of deep-sea exploration.

Chapter 2: "The Abyssal Residents"
2.1 Examination of the unique and bizarre creatures that inhabit the deep sea.
2.2 Profiles of bioluminescent organisms, giant squids, and other mysterious deep-sea denizens.
2.3 Discussion on the adaptations that allow these creatures to thrive in extreme conditions.

Chapter 3: "Lost Cities Beneath the Waves"
3.1 Exploration of ancient underwater civilizations and submerged cities.
3.2 Investigation of archaeological discoveries and the secrets they reveal about past civilizations.
3.3 Speculation on the reasons for the submersion of these once-thriving societies.

Chapter 4: "The Bermuda Triangle: Fact or Fiction?"
4.1 Analysis of the myths and legends surrounding the Bermuda Triangle.
4.2 Examination of real-life disappearances and mysterious phenomena in the region.
4.3 Scientific explanations for the occurrences and dispelling common misconceptions.

Chapter 5: "Shipwrecks and Sunken Treasures"
5.1 Exploration of famous shipwrecks and lost treasures hidden in the deep sea.

5.2 Accounts of successful underwater archaeology and salvage operations.

5.3 Discussion on the ethical considerations and challenges of preserving maritime heritage.

Chapter 6: "Underwater Mysteries and UFOs"

6.1 Investigation of reported underwater UFO sightings and encounters.

6.2 Examination of government and military involvement in studying unidentified underwater objects.

6.3 Discussion on the theories and speculations surrounding these mysterious phenomena.

Chapter 7: "The Future of Deep-Sea Exploration"

7.1 Overview of cutting-edge technologies used in deep-sea exploration.

7.2 Discussion on ongoing research and the potential for new discoveries.

7.3 Reflection on the importance of preserving the mysteries of the deep blue for future generations.

Conclusion

1

Introduction

The immense breadth of the dark blue ocean has charmed and enamored the human creative mind for quite a long time. Underneath the gleaming surface untruth secrets that coax us to investigate, to disentangle the mysteries concealed in the fathomless profundities. The sea, covering over 70% of the World's surface, stays a domain of mystery, a store of obscure miracles and perplexities. From the surface, the sea might appear to be an interminable region of water, yet underneath the waves lies a universe of intricacy that has long evaded our total comprehension.

As we set out on an excursion into the secrets of the dark blue, we end up defied with questions that have confused researchers, pioneers, and masterminds since the beginning of time. What mysteries does the sea hold in its quiet hug? What animals hide in the deep murkiness, and what variations permit them to flourish in conditions so not quite the same as those ashore? The sea, with its colossal tension, outrageous temperatures, and interminable dimness, presents difficulties that push the limits of our comprehension and test the constraints of human investigation.

One of the most persevering through secrets of the remote ocean is the unimaginable variety of life that exists in its apparently unwelcoming climate. From the tiny to the massive, the sea is abounding with organic entities that have developed to make due and flourish in conditions that would be deadly to most earthbound life. The disclosure of new species, a considerable lot of which oppose our assumptions of what life ought to be, proceeds to surprise and puzzle researchers. The remote ocean, specifically, is a hotbed of biodiversity, with innumerable species yet to be distinguished and considered.

As we dig into the profundities, we experience unusual and powerful animals that challenge how we might interpret science and advancement. Bioluminescent organic entities light up the obscurity with a hypnotizing show of varieties, making a dreamlike and outsider scene. From the spooky shine of the anglerfish to the throbbing light shows of jellyfish, the remote ocean is a domain of regular miracle that pushes the limits of what we imagined.

Past the entrancing showcase of bioluminescence, the remote ocean is likewise home to animals with unusual and captivating variations. From the gulper eel, with its expandable jaw equipped for gulping prey a lot bigger than itself, to the fangtooth fish, outfitted with teeth so enormous they can't close their mouths, the occupants of the profound have developed novel methodologies for endurance. These transformations bring up issues about the particular tensions that significantly impact life in the sea's profundities and the likely utilizations of these variations in fields going from medication to materials science.

While the remote ocean is a mother lode of natural variety, it is likewise a burial ground of depressed mysteries. Wrecks, lost urban areas, and old ancient rarities lie dispersed across the sea floor, ready to be found by fearless pilgrims. These submerged archeological destinations offer a brief look into the past, giving significant bits of knowledge into the historical backdrop of human civilization and the secrets of societies long neglected. The investigation of submerged paleontology not just uncovers the accounts of submerged boats and human advancements yet additionally brings up moral issues about the conservation and assurance of these lowered social legacy destinations.

As we explore the sea's profundities, we experience geographical peculiarities that shape the scene underneath the waves. Submarine volcanoes, aqueous vents, and submerged mountain ranges are only a couple of instances of the unique cycles that happen on the sea depths. The investigation of marine geography not just extends how we might interpret the World's interior cycles yet in addition holds the way to opening new energy assets and mineral stores. The investigation of these land highlights presents specialized difficulties that push the limits of designing and innovation, from remotely worked vehicles (ROVs) to independent submerged vehicles (AUVs) equipped for planning the ocean bottom in remarkable detail.

The secrets of the dark blue stretch out past the domains of science and geography to envelop the actual texture of the actual sea. Oceanography, the investigation of the physical and substance properties of the sea, uncovers the unpredictable interchange between flows, temperatures, and saltiness. The sea, when considered a static and perpetual span, is currently perceived as a dynamic and interconnected framework that assumes an essential part in managing the World's environment. Understanding the perplexing cooperations inside the sea is fundamental for anticipating environment designs, moderating the effects of environmental change, and guaranteeing the strength of marine biological systems.

However, even as we gain ground in disentangling the secrets of the dark blue, a large part of the sea stays neglected and obscure. The remote ocean, with its immense and blocked off profundities, presents difficulties that have prevented far reaching investigation. The outrageous strain, low temperatures, and nonattendance of light posture considerable hindrances to both human and mechanical investigation. As we push the limits of innovation and designing, new boondocks in sea investigation arise, offering looks into the obscure and opening ways to revelations that oppose our creative mind.

The mission to investigate the secrets of the dark blue isn't restricted to logical request alone; it additionally reaches out to the domains of folklore and fables. From the beginning of time, the sea has been a wellspring of motivation for stories of ocean beasts, mermaids, and lost developments. The appeal of the obscure, the boundlessness of the ocean, and the flighty idea of profundities have led to stories catch the human creative mind and fuel our longing for investigation. The sea, with its double nature of excellence and risk, stays an image of both interest and dread, typifying the embodiment of secret that keeps on bringing us into its hug.

In the cutting edge time, mechanical progressions have empowered us to investigate the sea in manners that were once unbelievable. Subs, remotely worked vehicles, and refined sensors permit researchers to look into the most obscure corners of the remote ocean and uncover its insider facts. Satellite innovation gives an elevated perspective of the sea's surface, checking changes in temperature, flows, and marine life on a worldwide scale. These apparatuses, combined with worldwide coordinated efforts and interdisciplinary examination, are changing comprehension we might interpret the sea and reshaping the account of investigation.

As we adventure into the secrets of the dark blue, we are defied not just with the miracles that lie underneath the surface yet in addition with the squeezing difficulties that compromise the wellbeing and supportability of the sea. Human exercises, from overfishing to contamination, are negatively affecting marine environments, prompting the debasement of coral reefs, the deficiency of biodiversity, and the development of no man's lands. Environmental change, driven by the consuming of petroleum products, is causing ocean levels to climb, sea temperatures to increment, and outrageous climate occasions to escalate, representing a danger to waterfront networks and marine life the same.

The earnestness of tending to these difficulties turns out to be progressively apparent as we perceive the interconnectedness of the sea with all parts of life on The planet. The sea, frequently alluded to as the "blue heart" of the planet, assumes a pivotal part in controlling environment, supporting biodiversity, and supporting human jobs. The fragile equilibrium of the marine climate is currently in danger, and the results of inaction are sweeping. As we investigate the secrets of the dark blue, we are likewise called to get a sense of ownership with its security and protection, to guarantee that people in the future can keep on wondering about the marvels that lie underneath the waves.

2

Chapter 1

"The Enigmatic Depths"

In the curious town of Eldoria, settled between moving slopes and old woodlands, there existed a particular peculiarity that had long charmed its occupants. Eldoria was prestigious for otherworldly atmosphere and the cryptic profundities lay underneath its surface. Ages of residents had murmured stories of stowed away insider facts, ethereal energies, and neglected domains that existed together with their day to day existences.

The core of Eldoria was its focal square, a clamoring center where locals accumulated to trade stories and offer the most recent happenings. It was here that an old narrator named Elysia spellbound the creative mind of both youthful and old with her stories of the baffling profundities. Elysia, with her silver hair and puncturing blue eyes, had survived many seasons and professed to have witnessed the secrets that hid underneath the outer layer of Eldoria.

As per Elysia, the mysterious profundities were not a simple similitude but rather an unmistakable reality that could be gotten to through a secret entryway. This gateway, she demanded, lay disguised inside the profundities of Eldoria's antiquated woods, monitored by supernatural animals and safeguarded by old spells. Few actually considered trusting her, excusing her accounts as the result of an overactive creative mind. In any case, a small bunch of brave spirits, drawn by the charm of the obscure, left on endeavors to reveal reality.

Among these valiant travelers was a young lady named Lyra. With her wild twists and voracious interest, Lyra had consistently felt a profound association with the secrets that wrapped Eldoria. Directed by Elysia's stories, she set out on a mission to track down the secret entrance and open the mysteries of the cryptic profundities. Outfitted with a guide that Elysia had drawn from memory, Lyra wandered into the core of the old woods, where daylight attempted to infiltrate the thick overhang.

The woodland was buzzing with murmurs, and the air was thick with a supernatural energy. Lyra went ahead, directed by an intuition that appeared to rise above the limits of customary discernment. As she dug further into the woodland, the trees surrounded her, making an ethereal passage that appeared to boundlessly extend. The air became colder, and abnormal images showed up on the bark of the antiquated trees, gleaming delicately in the faint light.

Following quite a while of persistent investigation, Lyra coincidentally found a clearing washed in a powerful sparkle. In the focal point of the clearing stood an old stone curve canvassed in greenery and ivy. As Lyra drew nearer, the air gleamed with inconspicuous powers, and the curve appeared to allure her forward. With a reluctant breath, she ventured through the gateway and felt a flood of energy wrap her.

On the opposite side, Eldoria changed into a strange scene of lively varieties and drifting islands. The laws of physical science appeared to twist, and the sky above was a material of twirling lights. Lyra wondered about the magnificence of this secret domain, understanding that the cryptic profundities were a legend as well as an equal aspect coinciding with her recognizable town.

In this strange domain, Lyra experienced creatures of unadulterated energy, ethereal animals that conveyed through considerations and feelings. They invited her as an explorer from the human domain and uncovered that the cryptic profundities were a combination point for different aspects, each with its own special qualities. Lyra, it appeared, had turned into an extension between universes.

As Lyra investigated the puzzling profundities, she found that the domain held antiquated information and intelligence that could reshape the predetermination of Eldoria. The ethereal creatures directed her through huge libraries of drifting books, each containing the amassed

insight of incalculable human advancements. She found out about the fragile harmony between the mysterious energies that pervaded Eldoria and the unmistakable world occupied by its residents.

In any case, as Lyra dug further into the mysterious profundities, she likewise revealed the presence of a noxious power that tried to take advantage of the energies for dull purposes. This power, known as the Shadow Weaver, snuck in the shadows of the enchanted domain, benefiting from the apprehensions and uncertainties of both the locals and the ethereal creatures. Its impact had saturated Eldoria, causing dissension and turmoil.

Still up in the air to safeguard her town, Lyra left on a journey to face the Shadow Weaver and reestablish the harmony between the domains. The ethereal creatures, perceiving her as the divinely selected individual, presented to her old ancient rarities and pervaded her with the ability to explore the mysterious profundities. Equipped with freshly discovered capacities, Lyra set off to confront the approaching danger.

The excursion was hazardous, loaded up with preliminaries that tried Lyra's purpose and resourcefulness. She experienced deceptions that played on her most profound apprehensions, crossed scenes that made no sense, and participated in fights against shadowy substances that tried to capture her. Through each test, Lyra developed further, taking advantage of the dormant potential that the perplexing profundities had opened inside her.

As Lyra moved toward the core of the enchanted domain, she felt the severe presence of the Shadow Weaver approaching ever bigger. The ethereal creatures cautioned her of the guile idea of this vindictive power, fit for controlling reality itself. Unflinching, Lyra went ahead, directed by an inward strength energized by her affection for Eldoria and its kin.

In the last a conflict, the confounding profundities appeared as a dreamlike war zone where reality itself appeared to crack. The Shadow Weaver, a shapeless element of murkiness, provoked Lyra with murmurs of uncertainty and despondency. Be that as it may, she, strengthened by the insight gathered from the mysterious domain, stood steadfast. With an eruption of energy, she released the power inside her, making a hindrance of light that repulsed the haziness.

The fight seethed on, a conflict of restricting powers that reverberated through the aspects. Lyra, using the antiquated antiquities presented to her, bridled the energies of the perplexing profundities to counter the Shadow all Weaver's moves. It was a fight of solidarity as well as of will, a challenge between the unadulterated goals of the divinely selected individual and the tricky maneuvers of the vindictive power.

As the contention arrived at its peak, the actual texture of the confounding profundities shuddered with the power of the battle. Eldoria, on the human plane, felt the resonations of the inestimable showdown. Townspeople detected a significant change in the magical energies that penetrated their environmental factors, as though the actual quintessence of the town was being reworked.

In a last, climactic flood of force, Lyra faced the Shadow Weaver with an old spell she had uncovered in the profundities. The chant, an amicable mix of mortal and ethereal dialects, resounded with the center of the supernatural domain. The very words appeared to rework the texture of the real world, scattering the obscurity and reestablishing harmony to the cryptic profundities.

As the last reverberates of the chant blurred, Eldoria went through a change. The town, when covered in secret, presently embraced a freshly discovered concordance between the mysterious and substantial domains. The old backwoods, as of now not a domain of stowed away mysteries, thrived with life and energetic energy. The ethereal creatures, thankful for Lyra's boldness, bid her goodbye, realizing that she had turned into an unbelievable figure in the embroidery of Eldoria's set of experiences.

Lyra, having satisfied her predetermination, got back to the town as a changed lady. The mysterious profundities, when a wellspring of vulnerability and dread, presently remained as a demonstration of the interconnectedness of various real factors. Elysia, the old narrator, welcomed her with a knowing grin, recognizing the job she had played in opening the secrets that had long enthralled Eldoria.

The townspeople, as well, embraced Lyra as a spanned the legend hole between their reality and the puzzling profundities. They praised her with celebrations and banquets, regarding the boldness that had saved Eldoria from the grasp of the Shadow Weaver. The town, washed in another light, flourished with a recharged feeling of solidarity and reason.

Thus, the story of the mysterious profundities turned into a valued legend in Eldoria, went down through ages. The focal square, when a center point of murmurs and hypothesis, presently reverberated with the giggling and delight of a local area that had figured out how to coincide with the magical energies that encompassed them. The town had been everlastingly changed, and the mysterious profundities had turned into an image of the indistinguishable association between the seen and the concealed, the known and the unexplored world.

1.1 Introduction to the mysterious world beneath the ocean's surface.

Underneath the gleaming surface of the world's seas lies a domain of unmatched secret and miracle — a tremendous region that envelops over 70% of the World's surface. The sea, frequently alluded to as the "last boondocks," harbors insider facts that have enraptured human creative mind for quite a long time. This presentation disentangles the perplexing scene underneath the sea's surface, investigating the profundities that have escaped our comprehension and welcoming you to plunge into the secrets that lie underneath the waves.

The sea, with its apparently vast skylines, has for some time been a wellspring of interest and motivation. Its profundities, stowed away from the relaxed spectator, contain an embroidery of life, scenes, and peculiarities that challenge the restrictions of human investigation. From the sunlit shallows to the inky darkness of the deep fields, the sea hides a huge swath of biological systems, each adjusted to the novel states of its specific profundity.

One of the characterizing elements of the baffling scene underneath the sea's surface is its sheer variety. The bunch of life frames that possess these profundities range from the littlest microscopic fish to the biggest whales, making an intricate and interconnected trap of biological systems. Coral reefs, with their dynamic tones and many-sided structures, have a kaleidoscope of marine life, while the untamed sea upholds transitory species that navigate huge distances looking for food and reasonable favorable places.

As we slip into the sea's profundities, the tension increments, and daylight decreases, giving way to a climate where transformation is the way to endurance. The mesopelagic zone, frequently alluded to as a twilight zone, is a domain where bioluminescent life forms produce their own light, making an entrancing showcase that enlightens the dimness. Here, weird and extraordinary animals, adjusted to the difficulties of low light circumstances, explore a world that seems outsider to surface-staying creatures.

Wandering much more profound, we experience the deep fields, where the strain is pounding, and temperatures float simply above freezing. In this cold climate, life has tracked down clever ways of flourishing. Strange and entrancing animals, like gulper eels and anglerfish, have developed exceptional variations to make due in the outrageous states of the remote ocean. The capacity to produce light, a peculiarity known as bioluminescence, becomes a scene as well as a method for surviving in the never-ending haziness.

The sea's secrets stretch out past the domain of science. Land highlights concealed underneath the waves recount an account of Earth's dynamic history. Submarine ravines, submerged mountain ranges, and aqueous vents are only a couple of instances of the geographical miracles that shape the sea depths.

These elements, frequently overflowing with life, offer a brief look into the intricate exchange between topographical powers and the development of marine environments.

The investigation of the sea's profundities has been a continuous journey for information and revelation. Progresses in innovation have permitted researchers and scientists to enter the murkiness and uncover the mysteries concealed underneath the surface. Subs, remotely worked vehicles (ROVs), and independent submerged vehicles (AUVs) have become fundamental devices in the journey to investigate the most profound spans of the sea. These innovative wonders empower analysts to concentrate on marine life, map the sea floor, and explore the geophysical cycles that shape the submerged scene.

Notwithstanding, in spite of our advancement, a significant part of the sea stays neglected. The most profound point on The planet, the Challenger Somewhere down in the Mariana Channel, arrives at profundities of more than 36,000 feet (10,994 meters), a spot so ungracious that a couple of monitored undertakings have slid to its profundities. The secrets of the chasm, the obscure animals that stay exposed and haziness, keep on evading our comprehension.

The sea's profundities are a domain of logical request as well as a wellspring of motivation for workmanship, writing, and folklore. From the beginning of time, the boundlessness and lack of definition of the sea have energized the human creative mind. Accounts of ocean beasts, mermaids, and secret developments underneath the waves have pervaded societies across the globe. The sea, with its consistently changing states of mind and unconventionality, has been both a dream and a similitude for the unexplored world.

As of late, a developing consciousness of the significance of the sea to the soundness of the planet has prompted expanded endeavors to study and safeguard this delicate biological system. Environmental change, contamination, overfishing, and territory annihilation compromise the fragile harmony between marine life and biological systems. The need to comprehend and monitor the sea has never been really squeezing, as its wellbeing is naturally connected to the prosperity of the whole planet.

The secretive world underneath the sea's surface isn't just a demonstration of the marvels of the regular world yet in addition a sign of the interconnectedness of all life on The planet. The sea, with flows course intensity and supplements, assumes a vital part in controlling the planet's environment. The fragile equilibrium of marine environments impacts atmospheric conditions, supports fisheries that feed billions of individuals, and adds to the oxygen we relax.

As we leave on this excursion into the perplexing profundities of the sea, let us approach with a feeling of miracle and modesty. The sea, regardless of its immeasurability, is a delicate environment that requires our figuring out, regard, and security. The secrets that lie underneath the waves are logical riddles to be tackled as well as a demonstration of the versatility and flexibility of life on The planet.

In the parts that follow, we will dig into explicit parts of the sea's secrets, from the unimaginable variations of marine life to the geographical marvels that shape the sea depths. We will investigate the mechanical developments that empower us to investigate the most profound scopes of the sea and the continuous endeavors to ration and support this indispensable environment. Together, let us disentangle the mysteries of the puzzling scene underneath the sea's surface, a world that keeps on rousing wonder and interest in the people who set out to investigate its profundities.

1.2 Historical overview of human fascination with the deep sea.

The human interest with the remote ocean is an embroidery woven through the chronicles of history — an excursion set apart by interest, fantasy, investigation, and logical disclosure. From the earliest civic establishments to the advanced period, the remote ocean has caught the creative mind of mankind, rousing investigation, imaginative articulation, and logical request. This authentic outline disentangles the strings of our getting through interest with the puzzling profundities of the sea.

In old times, the ocean was frequently seen with a blend of stunningness and fear. Early civilizations, subject to the abundance of the seas for food and exchange, created rich folklores and stories to make sense of the secrets that lay underneath the waves. The Greeks, for instance, trusted in ocean divinities like Poseidon, the lord of the ocean, and his mermaid-like specialists, the Nereids. These legends filled in as a manner to both honor and pacify the flighty powers of the sea.

As oceanic investigation extended, so too did the human longing to figure out the secret domains of the ocean. In the period of sail, nautical societies explored unknown waters, experiencing new terrains and experiencing abnormal animals that powered the creative mind. The stories of ocean beasts, for example, the kraken or the leviathan, arose as a method for making sense of the unexplained peculiarities saw by mariners. These legendary animals, with their monster size and strange nature, typified the feelings of trepidation and miracles related with the boundlessness of the sea.

The Renaissance denoted a defining moment in the human impression of the normal world, including the sea. During this time of scholarly and creative recovery, logical interest started to supplant strange notion. Spearheading masterminds, for example, Leonardo da Vinci and Galileo Galilei mentioned objective facts and portrayals that laid the basis for a more precise comprehension of the ocean. Notwithstanding, the profound sea remained generally unavailable, its secrets concealed underneath the surface.

The coming of remote ocean investigation in the nineteenth century denoted a huge jump forward in humankind's mission to figure out the sea's profundities. The HMS Challenger campaign, led somewhere in the range of 1872 and 1876, remains as a milestone throughout the entire existence of sea life science.

Outfitted with recently created innovations, including remote ocean examining gear and transmit correspondence, the Challenger endeavor investigated beforehand strange waters, revealing an abundance of data about the sea's geography, science, and science.

The Challenger undertaking uncovered a world overflowing with life, even in the haziest and most remote ranges of the sea. The disclosure of odd and beforehand obscure species caught public creative mind and ignited a restored interest in the secrets of the remote ocean. Logical diaries and famous media of the time reported the discoveries, encouraging a feeling of miracle and interest in the secret domains underneath the waves.

In the mid twentieth 100 years, the development of the bathysphere — a sub intended for remote ocean investigation — opened additional opportunities for concentrating on the sea's profundities. In 1930, the bathysphere slipped to a profundity of 4,500 feet (1,372 meters), giving scientists a firsthand perspective on the remote ocean climate. This obvious the start of another period in oceanography, as researchers acquired direct admittance to the profundities and could concentrate on marine life and geography right at home.

The mid-twentieth century saw the improvement of further developed subs and remotely worked vehicles (ROVs), empowering researchers to investigate considerably more profound and more difficult to reach portions of the sea. The Trieste, a bathyscaphe, plunged to the most profound point on The planet — the Challenger Somewhere down in the Mariana Channel — in 1960, arriving at a profundity of 35,797 feet (10,911 meters). This memorable accomplishment, combined with headways in sonar innovation and submerged photography, kept on revealing the secrets of the remote ocean.

As investigation extended, so did how we might interpret the interconnectedness of the sea and the planet's environment. The remote ocean, when thought about a remote and segregated domain, was uncovered to assume an essential part in controlling Earth's temperature and supporting the worldwide carbon cycle. The revelation of aqueous vents on the sea depths, environments supported by chemosynthesis instead of daylight, tested customary thoughts of where life could flourish.

Craftsmanship and writing have likewise assumed a huge part in molding the human interest with the remote ocean. Works like Jules Verne's "20,000 Associations Under the Ocean" and H.P. Lovecraft's "The Call of Cthulhu" have woven stories of experience and awfulness that dive into the secrets of the sea's profundities. Specialists like Winslow Homer and Hokusai have caught the heavenly magnificence and force of the ocean in their canvases, making notorious pictures that bring out the tremendousness and vulnerability of the sea.

The appeal of the remote ocean reaches out past logical request and creative articulation — it has likewise determined monetary pursuits and international interests. The journey for significant assets, like oil and minerals, has prompted expanded investigation of the sea floor. Countries with seaside domains strive for command over select financial zones, starting discussions over the protection and feasible utilization of marine assets.

In late many years, worries about the effect of human exercises on the sea have provoked a recharged center around marine preservation and ecological stewardship. Overfishing, contamination, environmental change, and territory obliteration compromise the sensitive equilibrium of marine biological systems. The remote ocean, with its remarkable and frequently sluggish developing species, is especially helpless against the tensions forced by human exercises.

The improvement of marine safeguarded regions, peaceful accords on fisheries the board, and endeavors to decrease plastic contamination address ventures toward a more economical relationship with the sea. Logical exploration keeps on assuming a significant part in illuminating protection strategies and advancing a more profound comprehension of the complicated collaborations inside marine biological systems.

The remote ocean stays an outskirts of investigation, with a lot of its huge span still unfamiliar and obscure. Continuous progressions in innovation, from independent submerged vehicles (AUVs) to refined sensors, keep on extending our capacity to study and screen the sea's profundities. The secrets that lie underneath the waves — whether in the haziest channels or the sunlit shallows — keep on charming the human creative mind and drive our aggregate mission for information.

All in all, the verifiable outline of human interest with the remote ocean uncovers a story of developing viewpoints, from legendary translations to logical investigation. The sea, when covered in secret and strange notion, has turned into a domain of logical disclosure, natural concern, and creative motivation. The excursion into the remote ocean is progressing, as humankind looks to open the excess mysteries of this tremendous and puzzling scope. The remote ocean, with its secrets and difficulties, keeps on coaxing us to investigate, comprehend, and protect the miracles that lie underneath the outer layer of the world's seas.

1.3 Brief exploration of uncharted territories and the challenges of deep-sea exploration.

The investigation of strange domains, especially the remote ocean, has for some time been a pursuit that spellbinds the human soul and energizes our natural interest. The huge breadths of the sea depths, concealed underneath layers of water and dimness, address one of the keep going boondocks on The planet. This investigation isn't without its difficulties, as the outrageous states of the remote ocean present special deterrents that require creative arrangements and state of the art innovation.

The strange regions of the remote ocean are in many cases portrayed by their distance, obscurity, and outrageous tension. While the outer layer of the sea is washed in daylight, considering photosynthesis and supporting a different cluster of life, the more deeply districts are covered in ceaseless murkiness. The shortfall of daylight represents a test for creatures that depend on photosynthesis, prompting the development of exceptional environments that rely upon elective energy sources, like chemosynthesis.

The outrageous tension in the remote ocean is an outcome of the heaviness of the water section above. Each 33 feet (10 meters) of profundity adds an extra air of tension, compacting the climate and making it cold for some organic entities adjusted to the surface. At the most profound point on The planet, the Challenger Somewhere down in the Mariana Channel, the tension surpasses multiple times that at the surface — a condition that presents impressive difficulties for both living organic entities and the innovation utilized in remote ocean investigation.

The distance of these unfamiliar regions adds one more layer of intricacy to investigation. The limitlessness of the sea, combined with the impediments of human perseverance and innovation, implies that huge parts of the remote ocean remain generally neglected. Just a negligible portion of the sea depths has been planned with high goal, leaving a lot of it as a fresh start holding on to uncover its privileged insights.

The difficulties of investigating unfamiliar domains in the remote ocean have not hindered researchers and travelers. All things being equal, these difficulties have prodded the advancement of progressively refined apparatuses and innovations intended to explore the intricacies of the sea's profundities. Submarines, remotely worked vehicles (ROVs), and independent submerged vehicles (AUVs) are among the key instruments that have empowered people to broaden their venture into the remote ocean.

Submarines, monitored vehicles intended to convey people to outrageous profundities, play had a noteworthy impact in remote ocean investigation. The bathysphere, a circular submarine with a built up steel body, was among the principal vehicles to permit people to plunge into the sea's profundities. The Trieste, a bathyscaphe, arrived at the Challenger Somewhere down in 1960, establishing a standard for the most profound monitored plunge that held for a long time.

While monitored submarines have given a remarkable viewpoint and considered direct perception of the remote ocean, they are restricted with regards to profundity, perseverance, and the quantity of people they can oblige. Remotely worked vehicles (ROVs) address a portion of these impediments by permitting administrators to control the vehicle from the surface. Furnished with cameras, sensors, and controller arms, ROVs give a way to investigate the remote ocean with more noteworthy accuracy and flexibility.

Independent submerged vehicles (AUVs) address one more mechanical headway in remote ocean investigation. Dissimilar to ROVs, AUVs work freely, following pre-modified ways and gathering information without direct human control. These vehicles are furnished with different sensors, including sonar, cameras, and compound analyzers, permitting them to review huge regions and assemble significant data about the sea depths and water section.

One of the remarkable difficulties looked by these innovative wonders is the outrageous tension of the remote ocean. Planning vehicles that can endure the devastating tensions at incredible profundities requires designing skill and materials equipped for enduring gigantic powers. The improvement of particular materials, for example, high-strength combinations and polymers, has been pivotal in making vehicles that can endure the extreme states of the profound sea.

One more snag in the investigation of unknown regions is the requirement for exact planning of the sea floor. Until somewhat as of late, a significant part of the remote ocean was planned utilizing reverberation sounding, a method that actions the time it takes for sound waves to venture out from a boat to the ocean bottom and back. While successful for fundamental planning, this technique misses the mark on goal expected to uncover the definite elements of the sea depths.

Ongoing progressions in planning innovation, for example, multibeam sonar and satellite altimetry, have enormously worked on our capacity to plan the geography of the sea floor. Multibeam sonar frameworks utilize a variety of sensors to quantify the profundity of the ocean bottom across a wide area, giving high-goal bathymetric information. Satellite altimetry utilizes satellite estimations of ocean surface level to deduce the basic geography, offering a worldwide viewpoint on sea depths highlights.

In spite of these mechanical advances, the remote ocean keeps on presenting difficulties that require continuous development. Correspondence is one such test, as communicating information from the profundities of the sea to the surface progressively can be thwarted by the water's conductivity and the distance in question. Creating solid correspondence frameworks is vital for remotely worked vehicles and independent submerged vehicles to hand-off data to administrators on a superficial level.

Natural testing in the remote ocean is another region that presents special difficulties. The fragile idea of remote ocean organic entities and the requirement for accuracy in gathering tests require particular devices and procedures. Attractions samplers, coring gadgets, and controller arms on ROVs are among the instruments used to gather examples without causing harm. Saving these examples for study upon recovery is likewise a basic part of remote ocean investigation.

The disclosure of aqueous vents in the late twentieth century represents the astonishments that anticipate in unfamiliar regions of the remote ocean. Aqueous vents are crevices in the sea floor where hot, mineral-rich liquids regurgitate into the chilly seawater, making extraordinary biological systems. These conditions, beforehand obscure to science, support an assortment of living things adjusted to outrageous circumstances, including tube worms, goliath mollusks, and eyeless shrimp.

The investigation of aqueous vents has given experiences into the possibility to life past Earth. The revelation of environments flourishing without daylight, depending on chemosynthesis rather than photosynthesis, extended how we might interpret where life can exist. Similar to conditions on different planets and moons, like Jupiter's moon Europa, have powered hypothesis about the chance of extraterrestrial life.

While mechanical headways have opened new outskirts in remote ocean investigation, the difficulties continue. The expense of creating, keeping up with, and sending progressed vehicles and instruments is a critical obstruction. Research vessels furnished with cutting edge innovation, like the R/V Falkor worked by the Schmidt Sea Foundation, assume a critical part in supporting remote ocean investigation. These vessels act as stages for conveying subs, ROVs, and AUVs, empowering researchers to direct state of the art research in the sea's profundities.

Global coordinated effort is fundamental in defeating the difficulties of remote ocean investigation. The endlessness of the sea, the common idea of its assets, and the interconnectedness of marine biological systems require a worldwide methodology. Drives, for example, the Nippon Establishment GEBCO Seabed 2030 venture plan to plan the whole sea depths continuously 2030, depending on commitments from associations, scientists, and innovation designers all over the planet.

Natural stewardship and preservation endeavors are progressively significant contemplations in remote ocean investigation. The delicate environments of the remote ocean, frequently portrayed by sluggish development rates and low regenerative rates, are vulnerable to aggravations brought about by human exercises. Overfishing, remote ocean mining, and the effects of environmental change present dangers to the sensitive equilibrium of these biological systems.

The Assembled Countries Show on the Law of the Ocean (UNCLOS) oversees the utilization of the world's seas and incorporates arrangements for the insurance and safeguarding of the marine climate. The Global Seabed Authority (ISA) controls remote ocean mining exercises in worldwide waters, looking to adjust the financial capability of mineral assets with ecological protections. Finding some kind of harmony between the advantages of asset double-dealing and the safeguarding of biodiversity stays an intricate test.

All in all, the investigation of unfamiliar regions in the remote ocean is a continuous experience that mixes logical request, mechanical advancement, and ecological stewardship. The appeal of finding new species, opening land secrets, and acquiring experiences into the essential cycles of life on Earth keeps on driving investigation endeavors. While the difficulties of outrageous strain, haziness, and distance continue, human resourcefulness and cooperative endeavors have opened remarkable windows into the secrets of the sea's profundities. The unfamiliar domains of the remote ocean, with their secret marvels and potential for notable revelations, stay a demonstration of the getting through soul of investigation that characterizes mankind's relationship with the normal world.

The difficulties of remote ocean investigation are diverse, enveloping a range of deterrents that reach from the innovative to the natural. As mankind tries to reveal the secrets of the sea's profundities, it stands up to the cruel real factors of outrageous tension, interminable dimness, far off areas, and the complex equilibrium of delicate biological systems. This investigation is a demonstration of human resourcefulness, however likewise an excursion laden with intricacies request creative arrangements and a profound comprehension of the one of a kind circumstances winning in the deep domains.

The fact that increases with profundity makes one of the essential difficulties in remote ocean investigation the persistent tension. The heaviness of the water segment applies gigantic power on anything plunging underneath the surface, establishing a climate where tension can arrive at stunning levels. Each 33 feet (10 meters) of profundity adds one more climate of strain, making the remote ocean a domain where the powers can pulverize. This represents an imposing test for the plan and designing of subs, remotely worked vehicles (ROVs), and independent submerged vehicles (AUVs) that should endure these outrageous circumstances.

Mechanical advancement has been urgent in beating the difficulties presented by tension in the remote ocean. Submarines, intended for monitored investigation, utilize strong materials and designing methods to make pressure-safe frames. The Trieste, a spearheading bathyscaphe that arrived at the most profound point on The planet — the Challenger Somewhere down in the Mariana Channel — utilized a mix of steel and gas filled tanks to accomplish lightness while enduring the extreme tension. Be that as it may, even with innovative headways, arriving at the most profound pieces of the sea stays an imposing endeavor.

Remotely worked vehicles (ROVs) and independent submerged vehicles (AUVs) address a portion of the impediments of monitored submarines. These automated vehicles are planned with pressure-safe lodgings, permitting them to endure the outrageous states of the remote ocean. ROVs, fastened to a surface vessel, can arrive at huge profundities and communicate ongoing information, while AUVs work freely, following pre-customized courses and gathering significant data about the sea depths. Notwithstanding these mechanical accomplishments, pressure stays a basic thought in the plan and activity of remote ocean investigation devices.

The interminable murkiness that covers the remote ocean presents another critical test. Dissimilar to the sufficiently bright surface waters that consider photosynthesis and backing a rich variety of life, the more deeply locales of the sea depend on elective energy sources. Without a trace of daylight, life forms in these domains have adjusted to outfit substance energy through processes like chemosynthesis. Investigating these dim conditions requests specific hardware furnished with cutting edge lighting frameworks, cameras, and sensors fit for catching pictures and information in low-light circumstances.

The difficulties of obscurity additionally stretch out to the trouble of route and direction without any noticeable milestones. While cutting edge sonar frameworks help with planning the geology of the sea depths, the shortfall of normal light makes it trying to position and move vehicles unequivocally. Procedures, for example, acoustic situating and inertial route frameworks have been created to upgrade the exactness of route in the remote ocean. In any case, the consistent haziness stays a key impediment that requires progressing mechanical developments.

Distance and detachment portray numerous unfamiliar regions in the remote ocean. Huge stretches of the sea depths stay past the span of customary investigation techniques, and the strategic difficulties related with arriving at these far off areas are extensive. The boundlessness of the sea, combined with the limits of human perseverance and innovation, has prompted huge bits of the remote ocean being generally neglected. Expeditionary endeavors are much of the time obliged by the requirement for research vessels, which act as stages for conveying subs, ROVs, and AUVs.

These examination vessels, outfitted with cutting edge innovation, are basic for remote ocean investigation. Notwithstanding, their accessibility, cost, and the time expected for expanded journeys present critical difficulties. Progressing drives, for example, the Nippon Establishment GEBCO Seabed 2030 task, try to resolve the issue of sea floor planning by utilizing global coordinated effort. These endeavors plan to make a complete and freely open guide of the whole sea depths continuously 2030, adding to a more exact comprehension of strange domains.

Correspondence is one more test that arises during remote ocean investigation. Sending information from the profundities of the sea to the surface presents novel troubles because of the conductivity of water and the distance in question. ROVs and AUVs, working at critical profundities, need to transfer data to administrators on a superficial level continuously. The advancement of dependable correspondence frameworks that can endure the difficulties of the remote ocean is pivotal for guaranteeing the outcome of investigation missions.

Natural examining in the remote ocean is a nuanced challenge that requires accuracy and care. The sensitive idea of remote ocean living beings, frequently with slow development rates and low regenerative rates, requires particular instruments and methods for gathering tests without

causing harm. Attractions samplers, coring gadgets, and controller arms on ROVs are among the instruments used to gather examples for logical review. Protecting these examples for additional examination upon recovery is a basic part of remote ocean investigation.

Progressions in submerged acoustics have essentially worked on the capacity to concentrate on marine life in the remote ocean without direct contact. Acoustic observing permits researchers to follow the development of marine species, concentrate on their way of behaving, and gain experiences into the elements of remote ocean environments. Inactive acoustic checking, utilizing hydrophones to catch regular sounds, has turned into a priceless apparatus for concentrating on the vocalizations of marine vertebrates and the soundscape of the remote ocean.

The sensitive equilibrium of remote ocean environments adds a layer of intricacy to investigation endeavors. The sluggish development rates and low conceptive paces of some remote ocean living beings make them especially powerless against unsettling influences brought about by human exercises. Overfishing, remote ocean mining, and the effects of environmental change present dangers to the sensitive equilibrium of these biological systems. Finding some kind of harmony between the advantages of asset abuse and the protection of biodiversity is a continuous test that requires global collaboration and insightful administration procedures.

Remote ocean mining, specifically, has arisen as a wellspring of both possible monetary increase and ecological concern. The rich stores of minerals, for example, polymetallic knobs, polymetallic sulfides, and cobalt-rich ferromanganese hulls on the sea depths hold the commitment of important assets. Notwithstanding, the extraction of these minerals can bring about territory annihilation, silt tufts, and the arrival of possibly hurtful substances. The Global Seabed Authority (ISA) supervises remote ocean mining exercises in worldwide waters, trying to lay out a system that offsets monetary interests with natural safeguarding.

Environmental change acquaints one more layer of intricacy with the difficulties of remote ocean investigation. Climbing ocean temperatures, sea fermentation, and changes in flows can have flowing consequences for marine environments. Understanding the effects of environmental change on remote ocean organic entities and biological systems requires long haul observing and interdisciplinary exploration. The remote ocean, in spite of its distant nature, is unpredictably associated with the more extensive examples of environment and sea course.

The climax of these difficulties highlights the requirement for an incorporated and interdisciplinary way to deal with remote ocean investigation. Joint effort between researchers, architects, hippies, and policymakers is fundamental for creating comprehensive techniques that address both the mechanical and environmental parts of investigation. The fragile harmony between human interest, mechanical advancement, and natural stewardship will decide the direction of future investigation endeavors in the remote ocean.

Taking everything into account, the difficulties of remote ocean investigation are imposing yet conquerable. Mechanical progressions have permitted humankind to push the limits of investigation and gain remarkable bits of knowledge into the secret domains underneath the sea's surface. As we keep on uncovering the secrets of unfamiliar regions, it is basic to move toward investigation with a significant regard for the fragile biological systems that occupy the remote ocean. Progressing endeavors in protection, reasonable administration, and global joint effort will shape the eventual fate of remote ocean investigation, guaranteeing that the miracles of the deep domains are both perceived and saved for a long time into the future.

3

Chapter 2

"The Abyssal Residents"

In the profundities of the sea, where daylight battles to enter the dim waters, lies a domain puzzling and unimaginable. This is the space of the Deep Occupants, an assortment of particular and perplexing animals that flourish in the outrageous tensions and never-ending murkiness of the deep zone. In this dark and outsider world, life takes on unusual structures, adjusted to the cruel circumstances that characterize their reality.

The deep zone, otherwise called the abyssopelagic zone, starts at profundities of around 4,000 meters and stretches out down to the sea floor, which can arrive at profundities of north of 11,000 meters in certain channels. The colossal strain, nonattendance of light, and freezing temperatures make this climate one of the most outrageous on The planet. However, despite everything, life perseveres in these profound, premonition waters.

One of the most notable and secretive occupants of the chasm is the anglerfish. The anglerfish is an expert of variation, furnished with an exceptional draw that hangs before its mouth like a bioluminescent casting pole. This bait, which produces a shocking gleam, draws in clueless prey in the inky haziness. The anglerfish's jaw is pivoted, permitting it to open wide and consume prey a lot bigger than itself. Its capacity to flourish in such outrageous circumstances is a demonstration of the flexibility and creativity of deep life.

The deep plain, a tremendous spread of level, featureless ocean bottom, is home to a bunch of animals uniquely adjusted to this dreary climate. Monster isopods, looking like curiously large woodlice, leave along the sea depths, benefiting from the garbage that gradually slides from the surface. These scavengers have fostered an inability to burn calories, permitting them to make due on the scant supplements that arrive at the deep profundities.

As one digs further into the void, the occupants become progressively odd. The gulper eel, with distensible stomach permits it to swallow prey a lot bigger than itself, is a great representation. This eel, otherwise called the pelican eel, utilizes its colossal mouth to overwhelm prey in the dimness, where finding food is frequently troublesome. The gulper eel's long, whip-like tail helps with route through the water, and its enormous mouth fills in as a demonstration of the difficulties of endurance in the void.

Remote ocean jellyfish, with their clear bodies and fragile arms, float smoothly through the deep waters. These ethereal animals have advanced to flourish in a climate where perceivability is restricted. Bioluminescent transformations permit them to deliver their own light, making a powerful presentation that enlightens the dimness. The jellyfish's capacity to throb and move with effortlessness without natural milestones is a demonstration of the exceptional versatility of deep life.

The deep occupants likewise incorporate species that challenge how we might interpret life's cutoff points. The goliath tube worm, found close aqueous vents on the sea floor, frames a cooperative relationship with chemosynthetic microscopic organisms. These microorganisms convert synthetics from the vent liquids into natural mixtures, giving food to the cylinder worm. This one of a kind transformation permits the monster tube worm to flourish in a climate where daylight can't enter, and customary wellsprings of energy are missing.

Aqueous vents, crevices in the World's outside layer that heave hot, mineral-rich water, make desert springs of life in the deep profundities. These vents support flourishing biological systems that are free of daylight and photosynthesis. The creatures that occupy these outrageous conditions have created particular variations to tackle the synthetic energy delivered by the vents.

One of the most wonderful deep occupants close aqueous vents is the sasquatch crab. Named for its particular, long, shaggy hooks, the sasquatch crab is a scrounger that feeds on the microscopic organisms that develop on its hair-like setae. These microscopic organisms, thusly, acquire their energy from the synthetics delivered by the aqueous vents. The sasquatch crab's appearance is both striking and unconventional, exhibiting the resourcefulness of nature in making living things adjusted to the most extreme circumstances on The planet.

Deep life isn't restricted to the profundities of the untamed sea; it stretches out to the channels that dive much more profound into the World's covering. The Mariana Channel, the most profound region of the planet seas, arrives at a stunning profundity of roughly 10,994 meters. In these channel conditions, where tension is enormous and temperatures are close to freezing, life continues in structures that overcome traditional presumption.

The hadal snailfish, found in the profundities of the Mariana Channel, holds the record as the most profound dwelling fish known to science. This clear, spooky animal has adjusted to the outrageous tensions by having a coagulated body that permits it to endure the devastating power of the water. The hadal snailfish's capacity to explore the channels and get through conditions that would be deadly to most other fish is a demonstration of the versatility of life in the pit.

In the most profound openings of the pit, where light is nonexistent, bioluminescence turns into a pivotal transformation for correspondence and endurance. Numerous deep inhabitants have developed to create their own light through bioluminescent organs, permitting them to explore the obscurity, draw in mates, and bait prey.

The lanternfish, a little and bountiful remote ocean fish, is a striking illustration of a bioluminescent deep occupant. These fish have light-delivering organs called photophores, decisively put on their bodies to make designs that confound hunters or draw in prey. The entrancing light shows of lanternfish and other bioluminescent organic entities add to the puzzling and charming atmosphere of the deep profundities.

As innovation progresses, people are acquiring the capacity to investigate and concentrate on the pit more meticulously. Submarines and remotely worked vehicles (ROVs) outfitted with cameras and logical instruments have permitted scientists to catch phenomenal film of deep life. The pictures and recordings caught by these gadgets offer a brief look into a world that was once past the scope of human comprehension.

While the deep inhabitants have adjusted to their outrageous surroundings more than huge number of years, they are not resistant to the effect of human exercises. The remote ocean, when remembered to be an unblemished and immaculate domain, is currently confronting dangers from overfishing, remote ocean mining, and environmental change.

These exercises can possibly disturb delicate deep environments and jeopardize the novel and inadequately comprehended species that possess them.

Protection endeavors and capable investigation are significant to guaranteeing the safeguarding of deep life. The Global Seabed Authority, laid out under the Unified Countries Show on the Law of the Ocean, assumes a key part in controlling remote ocean mining exercises to limit their natural effect. Endeavors to lay out marine safeguarded regions and advance reasonable fishing rehearses are likewise fundamental in shielding the fragile equilibrium of deep environments.

All in all, the deep occupants address a noteworthy and different exhibit of life frames that have adjusted to the outrageous states of the remote ocean. From the anglerfish with its radiant bait to the hadal snailfish getting by in the devastating profundities of the Mariana Channel, these animals oppose our assumptions of where life can prosper. As mankind proceeds to investigate and comprehend the pit, it is basic to move toward these conditions with care and regard, perceiving the significance of safeguarding the puzzling and striking world that exists in the haziest corners of our planet.

2.1 Examination of the unique and bizarre creatures that inhabit the deep sea.

The remote ocean, a tremendous and strange domain that comprises the biggest biological system on The planet, stays one of the least investigated and grasped region of our planet. Secret underneath the outer layer of the sea, in obscurity deep profundities, lives a variety of remarkable and unusual animals that have advanced to flourish in outrageous circumstances. This assessment digs into the uncommon transformations and ways of behaving of these remote ocean occupants, revealing insight into the wonders that exist in a world to a great extent stowed away from human view.

The remote ocean is a tremendous and complex climate that includes different zones, each portrayed by unambiguous physical and substance conditions. The daylight driven course of photosynthesis, which frames the premise of life in surface waters, becomes unfeasible in the profundities where daylight can't enter. Thus, remote ocean life depends on elective wellsprings of energy, frequently got from the waste that gradually sinks from the surface, or from the exceptional cycles related with aqueous vents and cold leaks.

One of the notorious and baffling natives of the remote ocean is the anglerfish. These puzzling animals are known for their particular bioluminescent draw, which hangs before their mouths like a casting pole. The bioluminescence is delivered by particular microorganisms living in the anglerfish's bait, making a frightful shine that draws in prey in the obscurity.

The anglerfish's transformation to the completely dark climate isn't restricted to its brilliant bait; it likewise has enormous, sharp teeth and a pivoted jaw that permits it to consume prey a lot bigger than itself. This mix of particular highlights empowers the anglerfish to explore the deep profundities with noteworthy productivity.

Diving further into the deep plain, a tremendous territory of level ocean bottom, one experiences an unconventional animal known as the monster isopod. Looking like a larger than average woodlouse, the goliath isopod is very much adjusted to the unforgiving states of the remote ocean. Its inability to burn calories permits it to get by on the restricted supplements that arrive at the deep profundities, and its searching way of behaving guarantees that it capitalizes on the irregular convergence of natural matter. The monster isopod's capacity to endure the outrageous tension and shortage of assets in the deep plain features the versatility and cleverness of remote ocean life.

The gulper eel, or pelican eel, is one more charming inhabitant of the remote ocean. With a long, snake-like body and a lopsidedly enormous mouth, the gulper eel has adjusted to the difficulties of tracking down food in the obscurity. Its distensible stomach permits it to swallow prey a lot bigger than itself, giving a vital benefit in a climate where food might be scant. The gulper eel's capacity to bait and consume prey in the profundities embodies the clever fixes that advancement has delivered notwithstanding the deep difficulties.

Wandering into the deep zone close aqueous vents, where super-heated water plentiful in minerals is removed from the World's inside, uncovers an exceptional and flourishing biological system. The monster tube worm, a meaningful occupant of aqueous vent conditions, frames a harmonious relationship with chemosynthetic microscopic organisms. These microorganisms use the synthetic substances in the vent liquid to deliver natural mixtures, giving food to the cylinder worm. The goliath tube worm's transformation to a daily existence without any trace of daylight grandstands the wonderful variety of systems utilized by remote ocean living beings to saddle energy in capricious ways.

Aqueous vent conditions likewise have the sasquatch crab, an entrancing animal with long, hair-like setae covering its hooks. The sasquatch crab's setae are colonized by microscopic organisms, shaping a microbial local area that gets its energy from the synthetic substances delivered by the aqueous vents. This special transformation permits the sasquatch crab to flourish in a climate where conventional food sources are scant. The revelation of such particular and unconventional transformations in remote ocean organic entities stresses the significance of proceeded with investigation to unwind the secrets of the void.

Traveling much more profound into the maritime profundities, one experiences the hadal zone, which incorporates the most profound channels on The planet. The Mariana Channel, the most profound of these channels, is home to the hadal snailfish, an animal types that holds the record as the most profound dwelling fish known to science.

This clear and coagulated animal has adjusted to the extraordinary strain of the channel by having a body that can endure the devastating power of the water. The hadal snailfish's capacity to explore and get by in the outrageous states of the Mariana Channel features the persistence of life in the most unfriendly conditions on our planet.

Remote ocean jellyfish, with their ethereal appearance and bioluminescent presentations, add one more layer of interest to the deep profundities. These thick animals float smoothly through the water, utilizing their bioluminescence for light as well as for correspondence. In the murkiness of the remote ocean, where perceivability is restricted, bioluminescence turns into a critical transformation for drawing in mates, discouraging hunters, and tricking prey. The charming magnificence of remote ocean jellyfish fills in as a sign of the staggering transformations that have developed because of the difficulties of the chasm.

Bioluminescence is a typical component among some remote ocean creatures, adding to the hypnotizing light shows that describe the deep profundities. Lanternfish, little and bountiful remote ocean fish, have photophores — light-delivering organs — that make perplexing examples on their bodies. These examples fill different needs, from confounding hunters to drawing in likely mates. The capacity of lanternfish and other bioluminescent life forms to produce their own light adds a layer of intricacy to the remote ocean environment, where correspondence and route are much of the time covered in haziness.

Mechanical headways in subs and remotely worked vehicles (ROVs) have empowered analysts to investigate the remote ocean with remarkable detail. High-goal cameras and logical instruments mounted on these vehicles have caught pictures and film of remote ocean life, offering a brief look into a world that was once unavailable to human perception. As how we might interpret the deep profundities develops, so does our appreciation for the variety and versatility of the animals that call this secretive domain home.

While the remote ocean has for quite some time been viewed as a remote and perfect climate, it isn't safe to the effects of human exercises. Overfishing, remote ocean mining, and environmental change present dangers to the sensitive biological systems of the chasm. Protection endeavors and mindful investigation are fundamental to alleviate these dangers and guarantee the safeguarding of the interesting and inadequately comprehended species that occupy the remote ocean.

The Global Seabed Authority, laid out under the Unified Countries Show on the Law of the Ocean, assumes a critical part in managing remote ocean mining exercises to limit natural effect. Endeavors to lay out marine safeguarded regions and advance feasible fishing rehearses are essential to defending the delicate equilibrium of deep biological systems.

As humankind proceeds to investigate and take advantage of the assets of the remote ocean, a smart and informed approach is fundamental to forestall irreversible mischief to this unprecedented and indispensable piece of our planet.

All in all, the assessment of the exceptional and odd animals that occupy the remote ocean uncovers a universe of unrivaled variety and variation. From the anglerfish with its iridescent draw to the hadal snailfish flourishing in the profundities of the Mariana Channel, these remote ocean occupants challenge how we might interpret life's cutoff points. As we open the mysteries of the void through logical investigation and mechanical progressions, it becomes basic to move toward the remote ocean with modesty and obligation, perceiving the significance of protecting the marvels that exist in the haziest and most remote corners of our seas.

2.2 Profiles of bioluminescent organisms, giant squids, and other mysterious deep-sea denizens.

The remote ocean, an immense and baffling domain that is the biggest environment on The planet, is home to a plenty of interesting and strange occupants. Among these occupants are the bioluminescent living beings that enlighten the deep profundities with their ethereal gleam. These animals have developed the wonderful capacity to create light, an expertise that fills different needs in the ceaselessly dull world they occupy.

Bioluminescence is a far reaching peculiarity in the remote ocean, with numerous living beings utilizing it as a type of correspondence, cover, predation, or fascination of mates. The anglerfish, a notable occupant of the remote ocean, represents the utilization of bioluminescence for predation. Its bioluminescent draw, hanging before its mouth like a gleaming casting pole, baits clueless prey in the haziness. The anglerfish's capacity to create light through cooperative microbes on bait features the mind boggling transformations have advanced in the profundities of the sea.

One more entrancing illustration of bioluminescence in the remote ocean is found in the lanternfish, a little and bountiful remote ocean fish. Lanternfish have concentrated light-delivering organs called photophores, disseminated across their bodies in mind boggling designs. These examples serve different capabilities, including confounding hunters, drawing in mates, and baiting prey. The lanternfish's utilization of bioluminescence features the adaptability of this variation in the complex biological cooperations of the pit.

Remote ocean jellyfish, with their sensitive and clear bodies, likewise add to the entrancing light shows of the void. These thick animals produce bioluminescence to enlighten their environmental elements, helping with route and correspondence. The charming magnificence of remote ocean jellyfish fills in as a demonstration of the variety of life in the profundities and the significance of bioluminescence as a transformation for endurance in a dark climate.

Notwithstanding bioluminescent creatures, the remote ocean is covered in secret by slippery monsters like the enormous and cryptic goliath squid. The monster squid, referred to deductively as Architeuthis, is quite possibly of the biggest invertebrate on The planet, with examples arriving at lengths of up to 43 feet or more. Regardless of its gigantic size, the goliath squid has stayed a slippery and sometimes seen animal, abiding in obscurity and distant profundities of the sea.

The monster squid's subtle nature has energized hundreds of years of sea fantasies and legends. Its appearance in writing, from Jules Verne's "20,000 Associations Under the Ocean" to current stories of ocean beasts, has added a quality of persona to this remote ocean goliath. The main pictures of a living monster squid right at home were caught in 2012, furnishing researchers and the public the same with a brief look into the cryptic existence of this goliath cephalopod.

The variations of the goliath squid to remote ocean life are remarkable. Its colossal eyes, among the biggest in the collective of animals, permit it to recognize faint hints of bioluminescence in obscurity profundities. These eyes are adjusted to low light circumstances, giving the monster squid a particular benefit in its dark territory. The goliath squid's taking care of propensities include strong limbs equipped with suckers and toothed clubs, which it uses to catch prey in the profundities of the sea.

Diving further into the strange occupants of the remote ocean, the fangtooth fish is one more particular native adjusted to the deep profundities. In spite of its brutal name, the fangtooth fish is a generally little animal, normally estimating around six creeps long. What makes the fangtooth fish fascinating is its lopsidedly huge and sharp teeth, which are among the biggest comparable to body size in any fish.

The fangtooth fish's teeth are huge to such an extent that they can't close their mouths completely. These impressive teeth are a transformation to the cruel states of the remote ocean, where prey might be scant, and the capacity to catch and get food is urgent for endurance. The fangtooth fish's appearance is a demonstration of the outrageous variations that have developed in the deep profundities, where assets are restricted, and rivalry for endurance is wild.

In the profundities of the sea, where daylight can't enter, the remote ocean dragonfish arises as one more entrancing animal with novel variations. The dragonfish has a long, slim body and is known for its bioluminescent light organs. These light organs are decisively positioned along the dragonfish's body and help in correspondence, cover, and drawing in prey. A dragonfish animal varieties likewise can deliver red light, which is undetectable to some remote ocean animals and fills in as a type of secret correspondence.

The remote ocean dragonfish's capacity to radiate red light is worked with by a shade called rhodopsin, which is delicate to longer frequencies. This variation permits the dragonfish to impart and explore in the obscurity without alarming likely hunters or prey that may be delicate to more limited frequencies of light. The complexities of the remote ocean dragonfish's bioluminescence feature the refinement of transformations that have developed in light of the difficulties of life in the chasm.

In the outrageous profundities of the sea, aqueous vents establish novel conditions that help lively environments. These vent conditions are described by superheated water plentiful in minerals, making desert springs of life in the murkiness. The vent environment is home to different organic entities, including the Pompeii worm, which holds the title of the world's most intensity lenient creature.

The Pompeii worm dwells close aqueous vents on the sea depths, where temperatures can arrive at more than 176 degrees Fahrenheit (80 degrees Celsius). Notwithstanding these outrageous circumstances, the Pompeii worm has adjusted to flourish in the hot and mineral-rich waters. Its padded members, which stretch out from its cylinder like natural surroundings, are shrouded in an intensity safe bacterial mat that gives protection and security from the burning temperatures. The Pompeii worm's capacity to endure the serious intensity of aqueous vents features the limits to which life can adjust in the remote ocean.

The remote ocean climate isn't just described by its puzzling and uncommon occupants yet in addition by the difficulties it postures to scientists and voyagers. Innovative headways, like remotely worked vehicles (ROVs) and independent submerged vehicles (AUVs), have reformed our capacity to concentrate on the remote ocean. These vehicles outfitted with cameras, sensors, and examining apparatuses permit researchers to investigate the deep profundities and archive the entrancing life that flourishes in this secret world.

The investigation of the remote ocean has revealed uncommon disclosures, including the presence of remote ocean coral reefs that rival their shallow-water partners in biodiversity. These coral reefs, tracked down in chilly water conditions, give fundamental natural surroundings to various remote ocean living beings. The sensitive and unpredictable designs of remote ocean corals house different networks, adding to the rich woven artwork of life in the chasm.

While the remote ocean keeps on uncovering its mysteries, it is additionally confronting expanding dangers from human exercises. Overfishing, contamination, and environmental change present dangers to the delicate biological systems of the void. Preservation endeavors and capable administration are essential to safeguard the exceptional and ineffectively comprehended species that occupy these profundities. The foundation of marine safeguarded regions and global collaboration are fundamental stages in protecting the biodiversity of the remote ocean for people in the future.

All in all, the profiles of bioluminescent creatures, monster squids, and other strange remote ocean natives offer a brief look into the miracles of the pit. From the anglerfish with its sparkling draw to the tricky monster squid meandering the dull profundities, these animals challenge how we might interpret life in outrageous conditions. As innovation advances and investigation proceeds, the remote ocean stays a wilderness of revelation, giving experiences into the variety of life on The planet and the multifaceted transformations that have developed because of the difficulties of the chasm.

2.3 Discussion on the adaptations that allow these creatures to thrive in extreme conditions.

The remote ocean, with its immense spans and outrageous circumstances, presents one of a kind difficulties for the living beings that call it home. The occupants of the deep profundities have developed a bunch of transformations that empower them to flourish in a climate portrayed by extreme tension, unending haziness, and restricted food assets. This conversation will dig into the striking transformations showed by remote ocean animals, revealing insight into the brilliant methodologies that have developed to adapt to the outrageous states of the pit.

One of the key difficulties looked by remote ocean creatures is the huge strain that increments with profundity. In the deep profundities, tensions can arrive at values a few hundred times more noteworthy than at the surface. The variations of remote ocean creatures to these tensions are obvious in their physical designs and physiological cycles. For instance, the thick body of the hadal snailfish, which occupies the Mariana Channel, permits it to endure the devastating power of the water at outrageous profundities. The hadal snailfish's capacity to explore and flourish in conditions that would be lethal to most other fish grandstands the noteworthy transformations that have advanced to balance the impacts of tension.

The goliath isopod, an occupant of the deep plain, has likewise evolved variations to adapt to the high tensions of the remote ocean. Its exoskeleton gives an unbending design that offers insurance from the outer tension, while its inability to burn calories permits it to make due on the restricted supplements that arrive at the deep profundities. The monster isopod's capacity to flourish in a climate where strain is a predominant element features the significance of physiological transformations in remote ocean endurance.

Temperature is one more basic calculate the remote ocean climate, with temperatures frequently close to freezing in the deep profundities. The fangtooth fish, in spite of its little size, has advanced variations to adapt to the crisp circumstances. Its smoothed out body decreases obstruction as it travels through the virus water, and its enormous pectoral blades help in keeping up with dependability. These physical transformations empower the fangtooth fish to effectively explore the bone chilling waters of the remote ocean.

In aqueous vent conditions, where temperatures can be particularly high, creatures, for example, the Pompeii worm have created one of a kind variations to flourish in the outrageous intensity. The Pompeii worm's padded limbs are canvassed in an intensity safe bacterial mat that goes about as protection, permitting the worm to live in closeness to the superheated water exuding from the aqueous vents. This variation shows the ability to strike of remote ocean life forms to take advantage of outrageous natural circumstances.

The shortfall of daylight in the remote ocean climate presents a critical test for living beings that depend on photosynthesis for energy. Without daylight, life in the void should rely upon elective wellsprings of energy. Aqueous vents and cold leaks give exceptional environments where life forms can outfit compound energy instead of sun powered energy.

The goliath tube worm, found close aqueous vents, frames a harmonious relationship with chemosynthetic microorganisms. These microbes use the synthetics in the vent liquid to create natural mixtures, giving a wellspring of food to the cylinder worm. This variation permits the monster tube worm to flourish in a climate where customary wellsprings of energy are scant. The advancement of chemosynthesis as an elective energy source highlights the flexibility of life in the remote ocean.

Bioluminescence is a pervasive transformation in the remote ocean climate, where obscurity wins. Bioluminescent creatures utilize light-delivering synthetic compounds to produce their own brightening, filling different needs like correspondence, predation, and mating. The anglerfish's bioluminescent draw, for example, draws in prey in the obscurity, giving the fish an unmistakable benefit in catching food.

The remote ocean dragonfish, with its light-delivering organs decisively positioned along its body, involves bioluminescence for correspondence and drawing in mates. The capacity to deliver light in different examples and varieties permits remote ocean organic entities to explore, impart, and collaborate in a climate where perceivability is generally restricted. The dependence on bioluminescence as an essential transformation features the job of light in the complex biological connections of the void.

Vision is a urgent sense in the remote ocean, where distinguishing faint hints of bioluminescence can be fundamental for endurance. The monster squid, with its gigantic eyes, has transformations that empower it to distinguish bioluminescent light in the haziness. The size and design of the goliath squid's eyes permit it to catch even the slightest hints of light, giving a particular benefit in the dark profundities.

Notwithstanding the difficulties presented by strain, temperature, and murkiness, the remote ocean is additionally described by the shortage of food assets. Some remote ocean living beings have adjusted to this restricted accessibility of supplements by creating remarkable taking care of systems.

The gulper eel, for instance, has a distensible stomach that permits it to swallow prey a lot bigger than itself. This variation is essential for catching prey in a climate where food might be rare.

The monster squid, an imposing hunter of the remote ocean, utilizes its strong limbs equipped with suckers and toothed clubs to catch prey. The versatility of the monster squid's taking care of systems permits it to explore the huge regions of the void looking for food. These taking care of variations highlight the significance of productive scrounging systems in the endurance of remote ocean living beings.

Multiplication in the remote ocean presents its own arrangement of difficulties, given the huge distances and low populace densities. The remote ocean dragonfish, for example, has created transformations for effective generation in the haziness. Females of some dragonfish species have bioluminescent organs that act as attractants, drawing likely mates in the dark climate. The capacity to involve bioluminescence for mate fascination is a basic variation for fruitful multiplication in the remote ocean.

While remote ocean organic entities have advanced momentous transformations to flourish in outrageous circumstances, they are not safe to the effects of human exercises. Overfishing, remote ocean mining, and environmental change present dangers to the sensitive biological systems of the void. Protection endeavors and capable investigation are urgent to relieving these dangers and guaranteeing the safeguarding of the one of a kind and ineffectively comprehended species that possess the remote ocean.

The investigation and comprehension of the remote ocean are progressing tries, with mechanical headways assuming a vital part in unwinding its secrets. Remotely worked vehicles (ROVs) and independent submerged vehicles (AUVs) furnished with cutting edge cameras and logical instruments have permitted analysts to investigate the deep profundities with remarkable detail. As our insight into the remote ocean grows, so does our obligation to safeguard and preserve this uncommon and delicate environment.

All in all, the variations that permit remote ocean animals to flourish in outrageous circumstances are a demonstration of the strength and resourcefulness of life in the pit. From the hadal snailfish with its coagulated body to the monster squid with its huge eyes, these variations address the staggering variety of techniques that have advanced because of the difficulties of the remote ocean. As humankind proceeds

MYSTERIES OF THE DEEP BLUE

to investigate and influence the void, a smart and informed approach is crucial for save the marvels of this secret world for people in the future.

The remote ocean, with its massive tensions, freezing temperatures, never-ending dimness, and scant assets, is a domain of limits that presents a bunch of difficulties for the organic entities that occupy its profundities. However, strikingly, the natives of the pit have developed a different exhibit of variations that empower them to flourish in conditions that would appear to be unfriendly to most life structures on The planet. This conversation digs into the surprising and brilliant transformations that these animals have created to make due, yet to succeed in the outrageous states of the remote ocean.

1. **Transformations to Strain:**
   The strain in the remote ocean increments decisively with profundity, arriving at values a few hundred times more noteworthy than at the surface. This represents a huge test for living beings, as the devastating power can misshape and harm their bodies. The hadal snailfish, found in the Mariana Channel, has developed a thick body that permits it to endure the colossal strain of the channel. This adaptable and compressible construction furnishes the hadal snailfish with the capacity to explore and flourish in conditions where most other fish would capitulate to the tension. The monster isopod, an occupant of the deep plain, has a hearty exoskeleton that gives a defensive safeguard against outer strain. This inflexible construction empowers the monster isopod to persevere through the high tensions of the remote ocean, offering a noteworthy illustration of how physical transformations can moderate the impacts of outrageous ecological circumstances.

2. **Adapting to Temperature Limits:**
   Temperature in the remote ocean shifts from close to freezing in the deep profundities to raised temperatures close aqueous vents. Creatures occupying these districts have advanced explicit transformations to adapt to these temperature limits.

The fangtooth fish, regardless of its little size, has smoothed out its body to lessen obstruction as it travels through the virus waters of the chasm. Enormous pectoral balances add to keeping up with security in the cold climate. This transformation exhibits the significance of physical designs in empowering remote ocean creatures to explore proficiently through their brutal environmental elements.

Conversely, the Pompeii worm, living close aqueous vents where temperatures can take off over 176 degrees Fahrenheit (80 degrees Celsius), has developed a remarkable technique to flourish in outrageous intensity. The worm's fluffy extremities are canvassed in an intensity safe bacterial mat, giving protection and security. The Pompeii worm's capacity to get through burning temperatures represents the assorted and concentrated transformations that have developed in light of the variable warm states of the remote ocean.

3. **Beating Obscurity:**

Never-ending obscurity portrays the deep profundities, representing a test for living beings that depend on vision for endurance. Bioluminescence, the capacity to deliver light, has arisen as a typical and essential transformation in the remote ocean.

The anglerfish, a notable occupant of the void, uses a bioluminescent draw to draw in prey in the dimness. The light is delivered by harmonious microorganisms living on the anglerfish's bait, thinking up a successful procedure for predation without a trace of daylight. The flexibility of bioluminescence for the purpose of drawing in prey features the genius of remote ocean creatures.

The remote ocean dragonfish, outfitted with light-creating organs along its body, involves bioluminescence for correspondence and drawing in mates. Some dragonfish species even radiate red light, imperceptible to some remote ocean animals, giving a secretive technique for correspondence. This exhibits how remote ocean living beings have saddled light as a device for route, correspondence, and predation in the dimness.

The goliath squid, with its gigantic eyes, has advanced a transformation to distinguish even the slightest hints of bioluminescence in its dark environment. These enormous and delicate eyes add to the goliath squid's capacity to explore and find prey in the remote ocean climate. The dependence on improved tangible insight, for example, huge eyes adjusted to low light circumstances, exhibits the specific tensions that have molded the advancement of remote ocean organic entities.

4. **Elective Energy Sources:**

Without any daylight for photosynthesis, remote ocean organic entities should track down elective wellsprings of energy. Aqueous vents and cold leaks, where mineral-rich water is ousted from the World's inside, make remarkable biological systems where chemosynthetic microscopic organisms assume a vital part.

The goliath tube worm, found close aqueous vents, shapes a harmonious relationship with chemosynthetic microbes. These microorganisms convert synthetics from the vent liquid into natural mixtures, giving a wellspring of food to the cylinder worm. This transformation permits the goliath tube worm to flourish in a climate where customary wellsprings of energy are restricted. The dependence on chemosynthesis as an elective energy source outlines the flexibility of life in the remote ocean.

5. **Proficient Searching Methodologies:**

The remote ocean climate is described by the shortage of food assets, expecting organic entities to foster effective scavenging systems. The gulper eel, with its distensible stomach, can swallow prey a lot bigger than itself.

This one of a kind transformation is critical for catching prey in the haziness of the void, where food might be rare. The gulper eel's capacity to adjust its taking care of conduct to the difficulties of its current circumstance embodies the variety of scavenging techniques in the remote ocean.

The monster squid, an imposing hunter, utilizes strong limbs equipped with suckers and toothed clubs to catch prey. The flexibility of the monster squid's taking care of components permits it to explore the tremendous breadths of the void looking for food. This delineates how remote ocean living beings have developed particular taking care of procedures to adapt to the difficulties of finding and getting food in their current circumstance.

6. **Remarkable Conceptive Systems:**
Multiplication in the remote ocean presents difficulties, given the tremendous distances, low populace densities, and the requirement for fruitful mate fascination. The remote ocean dragonfish, for example, has created transformations for effective multiplication in the obscurity. Females of some dragonfish species have bioluminescent organs that act as attractants, drawing possible mates in the dark climate. The utilization of bioluminescence for mate fascination is a basic transformation for fruitful multiplication in the remote ocean.

7. **Protection Difficulties and Human Effects:**
While remote ocean organic entities have advanced striking transformations to flourish in outrageous circumstances, they are not safe to the effects of human exercises. Overfishing, remote ocean mining, and environmental change present dangers to the sensitive biological systems of the void. Protection endeavors and mindful investigation are significant to alleviating these dangers and guaranteeing the safeguarding of the remarkable and inadequately comprehended species that occupy the remote ocean.

The foundation of marine safeguarded regions and worldwide participation are fundamental stages in saving the biodiversity of the remote ocean for people in the future. The investigation and comprehension of the remote ocean are progressing tries, with mechanical headways assuming an essential part in unwinding its secrets.

8. **Innovative Progressions and Investigation:**

Innovative progressions, like remotely worked vehicles (ROVs) and independent submerged vehicles (AUVs), have upset our capacity to concentrate on the remote ocean. These vehicles, outfitted with cutting edge cameras, sensors, and examining devices, permit researchers to investigate the deep profundities and report the entrancing life that flourishes in this secret world. As our insight into the remote ocean grows, so does our obligation to secure and ration this uncommon and delicate environment.

All in all, the transformations that permit remote ocean animals to flourish in outrageous circumstances are a demonstration of the strength and resourcefulness of life in the void. From the hadal snailfish with its coagulated body to the monster squid with its colossal eyes, these variations address the extraordinary variety of systems that have advanced in light of the difficulties of the remote ocean. As mankind proceeds to investigate and influence the chasm, a smart and informed approach is crucial for protect the miracles of this secret world for people in the future. The remote ocean stays a boondocks of disclosure, giving experiences into the variety of life on The planet and the mind boggling variations that have developed in light of the difficulties of the pit.

Chapter 3

"Lost Cities Beneath the Waves"

Underneath the tremendous region of the world's seas lie privileged insights stowed away from natural eyes, secrets hidden by the profundities of the ocean. Lost urban communities, when flourishing cities, presently rest in quiet isolation underneath the waves, their accounts reverberating through time like murmurs in the current. These lowered metropolitan scenes hold the leftovers of antiquated human advancements, their loftiness and destruction lowered in the sea's hug.

The charm of lost urban areas underneath the waves has caught the creative mind of travelers, students of history, and visionaries the same. The journey to uncover these lowered fortunes has driven travelers to the farthest reaches of the Earth, where the sea disguises the leftovers of once-strong social orders. These depressed urban areas, presently stowed away from the surface world, act as windows into the past, offering looks at former periods and individuals who once called these submerged domains home.

One such mysterious city is Pavlopetri, settled off the shoreline of southern Laconia in Greece. Pavlopetri is certainly not a legendary Atlantis, however an unmistakable archeological site, tracing all the way back to the Bronze Age. Found in 1967 by Nicholas Flemming, this depressed city is accepted to be around 5,000 years of age. Its impeccably safeguarded design, complete with roads, structures, and patios, gives a depiction of a modern culture that flourished during when many regions of the planet were still in the grasp of ancient effortlessness.

As analysts dive into the profundities encompassing Pavlopetri, they reveal signs about the regular routines of its occupants. The format of the city recommends careful metropolitan preparation, with structures adjusted along roads and open spaces decisively positioned. This old city was not a random assortment of designs but rather a painstakingly planned local area, displaying a high level comprehension of engineering and city arranging.

The meaning of Pavlopetri reaches out past its design wonders. The city's presence challenges ordinary timetables of human civilization, pushing back the limits of what we are familiar antiquated social orders. Its depressed roads and structures act as a period case, saving a crossroads in history when Bronze Age societies were prospering in the Mediterranean.

Getting across the globe to the sun-doused waters of the Caribbean, one more lowered city uncovers itself — the incredible Port Imperial. When a clamoring privateer shelter and a famous cave of lewdness, Port Illustrious met a devastating destiny in 1692 when a strong tremor sent a critical part of the city into the ocean. Known as the "Wickedest City on The planet," Port Imperial was a safe house for privateers, privateers, and every conceivable kind of marine heels during the seventeenth hundred years.

The indented vestiges of Port Illustrious lie off the bank of Jamaica, a demonstration of the fleetingness of human undertakings. As submerged archeologists investigate the lowered leftovers of this once-notorious city, they uncover relics that illustrate the privateer culture that once flourished inside its walls. From bars and whorehouses to business sectors and shipyards, Port Illustrious was a lively center point of sea movement.

The submerged unearthings of Port Regal have uncovered an astounding exhibit of relics, including all around saved structures, wrecks, and regular things from the seventeenth 100 years. The city's abrupt submersion, combined with the extraordinary states of the Caribbean seabed, has made a submerged archeological site dissimilar to some other. Maybe time stopped right now of Port Regal's obliteration, freezing the city and its mysteries in a watery hug.

The lowered city of Thonis-Heracleion, lying off the shore of Egypt, presents one more dazzling story of antiquated wonder lost to the profundities. Known as Heracleion to the old Greeks and Thonis to the Egyptians, this once-prosperous city filled in as a flourishing port and a focal point

of exchange during the hour of the pharaohs. Thonis-Heracleion was the doorway to Egypt for unfamiliar boats, a clamoring city that associated the Mediterranean and the Nile.

The city's submersion, accepted to have happened in the eighth century BC, consigned Thonis-Heracleion to the domain of fantasy and legend. For a really long time, it existed exclusively in old texts and the minds of the people who knew about its glory. Nonetheless, in the mid 21st hundred years, submerged archeologists made a shocking disclosure — Thonis-Heracleion was not a legend but rather an unmistakable reality concealed underneath the waters of Aboukir Narrows.

As jumpers investigated the submerged vestiges of Thonis-Heracleion, they revealed a city frozen in time. Gigantic sculptures, unpredictably cut stelae, and the leftovers of a fabulous sanctuary devoted to the goddess Isis rose up out of the sediment. The city's lowered roads uncovered a very much arranged metropolitan format, with proof of a mind boggling organization of trenches and harbors.

One of the most striking finds in Thonis-Heracleion was the disclosure of a submerged boat stacked with treasures. The boat's freight held a store of relics, including gold coins, gems, and strict contributions. This submerged time container gave an interesting look into the clamoring sea exchange that once energized the city's thriving.

The submersion of Thonis-Heracleion has been credited to a mix of catastrophic events, including tremors and rising ocean levels. The city's continuous plummet into the profundities fills in as an impactful sign of the fleetingness of even the most imposing human accomplishments. Thonis-Heracleion's rediscovery adds another section to the historical backdrop of old Egypt, extending how we might interpret its oceanic associations and social impacts.

Daring to the sunlit shores of India, the lowered city of Dwarka coaxes wayfarers and archeologists the same. As indicated by Hindu folklore, Dwarka was the incredible realm of Master Krishna, a heavenly city accepted to have been established quite a while back. While Dwarka's presence was for quite some time consigned to the domain of folklore, submerged investigations off the shore of Gujarat have uncovered indisputable proof of a once-flourishing old city.

The submerged vestiges of Dwarka, found in the late twentieth 100 years, have started banters among archeologists, history specialists, and strict researchers. The lowered designs, including walls, support points, and antiques, line up with depictions of Dwarka in antiquated texts like the Mahabharata and the Puranas. The submerged city's format relates to the many-sided city arranging ascribed to Ruler Krishna's realm.

The disclosure of Dwarka brings up issues about the authentic premise of antiquated fantasies and the possible crossing points among folklore and prehistoric studies. While some view the lowered city as proof of a verifiable Dwarka, others approach it with alert, aware of the difficulties in convincingly connecting legend to the real world. No matter what the understanding, Dwarka's submerged vestiges offer a tempting look into the rich embroidery of India's social and strict legacy.

The charm of lost urban areas underneath the waves stretches out past the domains of history and folklore. In the cold waters of the Icy, the remaining parts of Franklin's lost endeavor lie covered in secret. Sir John Franklin, an English traveler, set forth in 1845 with two ships, the HMS Erebus and the HMS Dread, looking for the Northwest Section.

The undertaking expected to explore a famous ocean course interfacing the Atlantic and Pacific Seas.

Notwithstanding, the Icy, with its slippery ice and brutal circumstances, demonstrated unforgiving. The destiny of Franklin's endeavor became quite possibly of the best secret in oceanic history. For quite a long time, the whereabouts of the two boats and the destiny of the team stayed obscure, energizing hypothesis and investigation.

In 2014 and 2016, the disaster areas of both the HMS Erebus and the HMS Dread were found underneath the bone chilling waters of the Canadian Icy. The strikingly all around safeguarded condition of the boats, alongside the ancient rarities found inside, offered experiences into the difficulties looked by Franklin and his team. The chilly, dim profundities of the Cold Sea had defended the remaining parts of the campaign, protecting an unfortunate section in the journey for oceanic investigation.

The revelation of Franklin's lost campaign features the double idea of submerged investigation — revealing the victories and misfortunes of human undertakings. The Cold's frosty waters, distant from the sun-doused districts of Pavlopetri, Port Regal, Thonis-Heracleion, and Dwarka, hold a remarkable spot in the records of sea history. Franklin's lost boats act as time containers, revealing insight into the dangers looked by travelers who thought for even a moment to wander into the unforgiving polar oceans.

In the Pacific Sea, the destruction of the USS Indianapolis lays on the sea depths, a dismal demonstration of the human expense of war. The USS Indianapolis, a Portland-class weighty cruiser, assumed a significant part in The Second Great War, conveying parts of the nuclear bomb that would later be dropped on Hiroshima. Subsequent to finishing this mysterious mission, the boat was obliterated by a Japanese submarine on July 30, 1945, sinking quickly.

The team confronted unbelievable detestations as they anticipated salvage in shark-plagued waters. The sinking of the USS Indianapolis brought about one of the best sea calamities in U.S. history, with just a small portion of the group enduring the difficulty.

The specific area of the destruction stayed obscure for quite a long time, adding to the secret encompassing the destiny of the boat and its group.

In 2017, the destruction of the USS Indianapolis was found in the Philippine Ocean by a group drove by Microsoft fellow benefactor Paul Allen. The submerged campaign found the tragically missing boat as well as given conclusion to the groups of the individuals who had died. The disclosure brought the awful story of the USS Indianapolis back into the public awareness, helping the world to remember the penances made during wartime.

The lowered remaining parts of the USS Indianapolis act as a piercing remembrance to the ones who served on board the boat and the difficulties looked by the people who explore the unsafe waters of war. The sea, frequently a venue of contention and misfortune, holds the quiet reverberates of wartime forfeits, its profundities covering the tales of depressed vessels and fallen legends.

While the investigation of lost urban areas underneath the waves divulges the secrets of the past, it likewise raises moral contemplations and difficulties. The sensitive harmony between logical request and the protection of submerged social legacy is a subject of progressing banter inside the archeological local area. The submerged locales, whether antiquated urban communities or wartime wrecks, are vulnerable to ecological dangers, plundering, and accidental harm from human exercises.

Saving these lowered fortunes requires a multidisciplinary approach that consolidates archeological skill, mechanical development, and ecological stewardship. Progresses in submerged advanced mechanics, remote detecting innovations, and painless overview techniques have empowered analysts to investigate and archive lowered locales without hurting delicate conditions. The fragile dance among investigation and protection is fundamental to guarantee that these submerged miracles stay in salvageable shape for people in the future.

The investigation of lost urban communities underneath the waves stretches out past the limits of Earth, venturing into the domains of extraterrestrial investigation. On one of Jupiter's moons, Europa, researchers estimate about the chance of a subsurface sea underneath its frigid outside. The potential for fluid water on Europa brings up enticing issues about the possibility of extraterrestrial life.

While Europa's sea stays stowed away from direct perception, researchers assemble signs from the moon's surface highlights, including breaks, edges, and turbulent territory. These elements propose the powerful interaction between the frosty outside and the subsurface sea underneath. The investigation of Europa's subsurface sea addresses another outskirts in astrobiology, as researchers consider the expected tenability of this far off moon.

The equals between Earth's seas and Europa's subsurface sea welcome hypothesis about the potential for life past our planet. In the event that Europa harbors life, it would rethink how we might interpret the circumstances important for science to arise. The mission to investigate the profundities of Europa's sea includes planning modern space tests and instruments fit for entering its cold hull to look for indications of something going on under the surface in obscurity, freezing profundities.

As mankind examines the secrets of lost urban areas underneath the waves and the potential for extraterrestrial seas, the association among investigation and the human soul becomes obvious. The bait of the obscure, whether concealed inside the World's seas or in the cold territories of far off moons, allures pioneers to push the limits of information and understanding.

Lost urban communities underneath the waves act as tokens of the temporariness of human accomplishments and the flexibility of the regular world. Whether indented by cataclysmic events, the progression of time, or the assaults of war, these lowered scenes offer looks into the past, opening the insider facts of old developments and sea history.

As innovation advances and investigation techniques develop, the submerged domain keeps on disclosing its privileged insights. From the carefully arranged roads of Pavlopetri to the privateer pervaded roads of Port Imperial, from the magnificence of Thonis-Heracleion to the legendary realm of Dwarka, each lowered city recounts an extraordinary story. These accounts, written in the language of depressed ruins and protected antiquities, add to the embroidered artwork of mankind's set of experiences.

In the profundities of the sea, where daylight blurs and quietness rules, the lost urban communities underneath the waves anticipate revelation. They are the quiet observers to the back and forth movement of civilizations, the ascent and fall of domains, and the persevering through soul of investigation that impels mankind forward. As we look into the pit, we are helped that the secrets to remember the profound keep on calling, welcoming us to wander into the obscure and disentangle the privileged insights that lie underneath the waves.

3.1 Exploration of ancient underwater civilizations and submerged cities.

Investigation of old submerged developments and lowered urban communities reveals a charming embroidery of mankind's set of experiences hid underneath the waves. The charm of diving into the profundities of the sea to uncover the insider facts of former periods has energized the minds of travelers, archeologists, and antiquarians all through the ages. The lowered remainders of once-flourishing social orders act as time containers, safeguarding the design ponders, social antiques, and untold accounts of civic establishments lost to the progression of time.

One of the amazing submerged archeological locales is Pavlopetri, arranged off the southern shoreline of Laconia in Greece. Found in 1967 by Nicholas Flemming, Pavlopetri is an old city going back roughly 5,000 years to the Bronze Age. Not at all like legendary stories of depressed civic establishments, Pavlopetri is an unmistakable and very much safeguarded archeological site that challenges how we might interpret old metropolitan preparation.

The format of Pavlopetri uncovers a fastidiously planned city, with roads, structures, and yards organized in an organized way. This degree of metropolitan arranging recommends a high level comprehension of engineering and local area association during when many regions of the planet were still in the hold of ancient straightforwardness. As specialists investigate the lowered city, they disentangle the regular routines of its occupants and gain experiences into the social, financial, and social elements of Bronze Age social orders.

The meaning of Pavlopetri reaches out past its design wonders. It challenges regular courses of events of human development, pushing back the limits of our insight about antiquated social orders. The city's presence fills in as a window into a period when Bronze Age societies were prospering in the Mediterranean, offering an unmistakable connection to the past that was beforehand just known through verifiable texts and relics.

From the sunlit shores of Greece, we dare to the tropical waters of the Caribbean to find the lowered remainders of Port Illustrious, a once-famous privateer sanctuary. Port Imperial, situated off the shoreline of Jamaica, was a flourishing city during the seventeenth 100 years, known as the "Wickedest City on The planet." It was a shelter for privateers, privateers, and different marine heels who looked for shelter in its clamoring roads.

The city's destiny took a sensational turn in 1692 when a strong seismic tremor sent a huge part of Port Illustrious into the ocean. The indented vestiges of Port Regal proposition a brief look into a past period of sea wilderness and lewdness. As submerged archeologists investigate the lowered city, they reveal very much safeguarded structures, wrecks, and curios that illustrate the privateer culture that once flourished inside its walls.

The submerged unearthings of Port Regal have uncovered a different exhibit of relics, including regular things, weaponry, and remainders of

MYSTERIES OF THE DEEP BLUE

the city's foundation. The states of the Caribbean seabed, combined with the unexpected submersion of the city, have made a submerged archeological site dissimilar to some other. Port Imperial's indented roads and designs act as a frozen scene, safeguarding the turbulent and lively history of this scandalous privateer sanctuary.

Getting across mainlands toward the northeastern shore of Egypt, the lowered city of Thonis-Heracleion rises up out of the profundities of Aboukir Cove. Known as Heracleion to the old Greeks and Thonis to the Egyptians, this once-prosperous city was a clamoring port and a crucial focus of exchange during the hour of the pharaohs.

Thonis-Heracleion's submersion, accepted to have happened in the eighth century BC, consigned it to the domain of fantasy and legend for a really long time.

The submerged vestiges of Thonis-Heracleion, found in the mid 21st hundred years, recount an account of glory and social trade. As jumpers investigate the lowered city, they reveal monstrous sculptures, unpredictably cut stelae, and the remainders of a stupendous sanctuary devoted to the goddess Isis. The city's very much arranged metropolitan design, complete with waterways and harbors, gives important bits of knowledge into the sea associations and social impacts of antiquated Egypt.

One of the most noteworthy finds in Thonis-Heracleion was the disclosure of a submerged boat stacked with treasures. The boat's freight, including gold coins, gems, and strict contributions, offers a substantial association with the city's lively oceanic exchange. Thonis-Heracleion's submersion has been credited to a blend of catastrophic events, including quakes and rising ocean levels, featuring the weakness of even the most prosperous urban communities to the powers of nature.

Traveling toward the western shore of India, the lowered city of Dwarka entices adventurers and archeologists. As per Hindu folklore, Dwarka was the unbelievable realm of Master Krishna, a heavenly city accepted to have been established quite a while back. While Dwarka's presence was for quite some time consigned to the domain of folklore,

| 59 |

submerged investigations off the shoreline of Gujarat have uncovered unquestionable proof of a once-flourishing old city.

The submerged remains of Dwarka, found in the late twentieth 100 years, line up with portrayals of the legendary city tracked down in old texts like the Mahabharata and the Puranas. The lowered designs, including walls, points of support, and antiques, relate to the perplexing city arranging credited to Master Krishna's realm. The revelation of Dwarka brings up issues about the verifiable premise of antiquated fantasies and the expected convergences among folklore and paleohistory.

While some view the lowered city as proof of a verifiable Dwarka, others approach it with alert, aware of the difficulties in convincingly connecting fantasy to the real world. No matter what the understanding, Dwarka's submerged remnants offer an enticing look into the rich embroidery of India's social and strict legacy, giving an archeological scaffold among fantasy and history.

The investigation of lost urban communities underneath the waves stretches out past the domains of antiquated developments to envelop the investigation of wartime wrecks and the accounts of human penance. In the frosty waters of the Cold, the remaining parts of Franklin's lost campaign lie covered in secret. Sir John Franklin, an English pioneer, set forth in 1845 with two ships, the HMS Erebus and the HMS Fear, looking for the Northwest Section.

The Icy, with its slippery ice and cruel circumstances, demonstrated unforgiving. The destiny of Franklin's campaign became quite possibly of the best secret in oceanic history. For quite a long time, the whereabouts of the two boats and the destiny of the team stayed obscure, energizing hypothesis and investigation. In 2014 and 2016, the disaster areas of both the HMS Erebus and the HMS Dread were found underneath the freezing waters of the Canadian Icy.

The amazingly all around safeguarded condition of the boats, alongside the antiquities found inside, offered experiences into the difficulties looked by Franklin and his team. The chilly, dim profundities of the Cold Sea had defended the remaining parts of the endeavor, protecting a shocking section in the journey for sea investigation. The revelation of Franklin's lost undertaking features the double idea of submerged investigation — uncovering the victories and misfortunes of human undertakings.

In the Pacific Sea, the destruction of the USS Indianapolis lays on the sea depths, a grave demonstration of the human expense of war. The USS Indianapolis, a Portland-class weighty cruiser, assumed a significant part in The Second Great War, conveying parts of the nuclear bomb that would later be dropped on Hiroshima. Subsequent to finishing this mysterious mission, the boat was obliterated by a Japanese submarine on July 30, 1945, sinking quickly.

The group confronted unbelievable detestations as they anticipated salvage in shark-pervaded waters. The sinking of the USS Indianapolis brought about one of the best sea debacles in U.S. history, with just a negligible portion of the team enduring the experience. The specific area of the destruction stayed obscure for a really long time, adding to the secret encompassing the destiny of the boat and its team. In 2017, the destruction of the USS Indianapolis was found in the Philippine Ocean by a group drove by Microsoft prime supporter Paul Allen.

The submerged endeavor found the tragically missing boat as well as given conclusion to the groups of the individuals who had died. The revelation brought the unfortunate story of the USS Indianapolis back into the public awareness, helping the world to remember the penances made during wartime. The lowered remaining parts of the USS Indianapolis act as a powerful commemoration to the ones who served on board the boat and the difficulties looked by the people who explore the hazardous waters of war.

While the investigation of lost urban communities underneath the waves reveals the secrets of the past, it likewise raises moral contemplations and difficulties. The sensitive harmony between logical request and the conservation of submerged social legacy is a subject of continuous discussion inside the archeological local area. The submerged locales, whether antiquated urban communities or wartime wrecks, are powerless to natural dangers, plundering, and accidental harm from human exercises.

Saving these lowered fortunes requires a multidisciplinary approach that consolidates archeological skill, mechanical development, and ecological stewardship. Propels in submerged advanced mechanics, remote detecting advancements, and painless overview techniques have empowered specialists to investigate and archive lowered destinations without actually hurting delicate conditions.

The fragile dance among investigation and protection is fundamental to guarantee that these submerged marvels stay in salvageable shape for people in the future. As innovation advances and investigation strategies develop, the submerged domain keeps on divulging its insider facts. From the fastidiously arranged roads of Pavlopetri to the privateer plagued roads of Port Regal, from the loftiness of Thonis-Heracleion to the legendary realm of Dwarka, each lowered city recounts an exceptional story.

3.2 Investigation of archaeological discoveries and the secrets they reveal about past civilizations.

The examination of archeological revelations is an excursion through time, an interaction that uncovers the leftovers of past civic establishments and opens the insider facts of mankind's set of experiences. Paleohistory, as a discipline, looks to sort out the riddle of the past by inspecting curios, structures, and social follows abandoned by old social orders. Through careful removal and investigation, archeologists disentangle the narratives of civic establishments a distant memory, revealing insight into their accomplishments, battles, and the complexities of day to day existence.

One of the most famous archeological destinations is the city of Pompeii, frozen in time by the ejection of Mount Vesuvius in 79 Promotion. Pompeii, a flourishing Roman city situated close to current Naples, Italy, was covered under layers of debris and pumice, safeguarding its roads, structures, and, surprisingly, the frightful engravings of its residents. The careful safeguarding of Pompeii offers a remarkable window into the regular routines of old Romans, giving experiences into their engineering, craftsmanship, and social designs.

The unearthings at Pompeii have uncovered a city of momentous complexity, complete with cleared roads, public structures, and confidential homes decorated with complicated frescoes and mosaics. The mortar projects of human bodies, trapped in the pains of their last minutes, bring out an instinctive association with the misfortune that happened to the city. The relics recuperated from Pompeii — utensils, stoneware, and ordinary things — offer a substantial look into the schedules and customs of its occupants.

Past the awfulness of Pompeii, archeological revelations in Egypt have uncovered the loftiness of antiquated human advancements along the banks of the Nile. The Valley of the Lords, a graveyard for pharaohs and aristocrats, contains burial places decorated with intricate pictographs and complicated canvases.

The revelation of Tutankhamun's burial chamber in 1922 by Howard Carter uncovered a mother lode of relics, including the celebrated brilliant cover of the youthful pharaoh.

The pictographs and engravings on the walls of these burial chambers give an itemized record of strict convictions, regal genealogies, and day to day existence in old Egypt. The pyramids, especially the Incomparable Pyramid of Giza, stand as stupendous accomplishments in design and designing, testing how we might interpret the capacities of antiquated civic establishments. The mysteries of these epic designs, built with accuracy and lined up with galactic peculiarities, keep on enthralling researchers and aficionados the same.

In the Americas, the archeological site of Machu Picchu in Peru remains as a demonstration of the resourcefulness of the Inca civilization. Worked on the Andes Mountains, this old city is prestigious for its modern porches, sanctuaries, and local locations. The design of Machu Picchu mirrors a cozy association between the Inca public and the normal scene, displaying progressed rural strategies and building ability.

The secrets of Machu Picchu reach out past its stunning landscape. The motivation behind the site, its development techniques, and the explanations behind its deserting remain subjects of academic discussion. The archeological examination of Machu Picchu offers a brief look into the cultural association and profound convictions of the Inca development, giving important experiences into their accomplishments and the difficulties they confronted.

Moving toward the east to the Indus Valley, the archeological disclosures at locales like Mohenjo-daro and Harappa shed light on one of the world's earliest metropolitan developments. Thriving around 2600-1900 BCE, individuals of the Indus Valley made arranged urban communities with cutting edge sterilization frameworks, block lined roads, and multi-story houses. The complicatedly planned seals found at these locales include a remarkable content that, until this point, stays undeciphered.

The absence of great engineering in the Indus Valley has filled banters about the idea of administration, social construction, and social practices in this antiquated development. The efficient design of urban communities and the high level designing of their water and seepage frameworks demonstrate an elevated degree of metropolitan preparation and innovative ability. Nonetheless, the abrupt decay of the Indus Valley Human advancement brings up issues about the elements that prompted its inevitable breakdown.

Investigating the Mediterranean locale, the antiquated city of Troy became amazing through the sagas of Homer. The archeological site of Troy, situated in advanced Turkey, has gone through broad uncovering, uncovering different layers of occupation spreading over millennia. The disclosure of the city's protective walls and the remaining parts of different designs lines up with the portrayals in the Iliad, giving substantial proof of the authentic reason for the Trojan Conflict.

The layers of Troy compare to various times of its set of experiences, permitting archeologists to follow the city's development and the effect of different societies, including the Hittites and Mycenaeans. The relics uncovered at Troy offer experiences into exchange organizations, mechanical progressions, and the social trades that formed the city throughout the long term. The examination of Troy embodies the cooperative idea of paleohistory, where authentic texts, legend, and actual proof combine to reproduce the past.

In the domain of oceanic paleontology, the depressed city of Pavlopetri off the shore of southern Laconia in Greece presents a lowered time container. Tracing all the way back to the Bronze Age, Pavlopetri is a surprisingly very much saved city with roads, structures, and patios, offering experiences into old metropolitan preparation. The submerged examination of Pavlopetri uncovers a modern culture that flourished during a period when many regions of the planet were still in the grasp of ancient effortlessness.

The meaning of Pavlopetri reaches out past its engineering wonders. The city challenges ordinary timetables of human civilization, pushing back the limits of what we are familiar old social orders. Its lowered roads and structures act as a period case, protecting a crossroads in history when Bronze Age societies were prospering in the Mediterranean. Pavlopetri features the capability of submerged paleohistory to change the story of mankind's set of experiences.

The investigation of lowered urban communities stretches out to the Caribbean, where the depressed remaining parts of Port Illustrious off the shore of Jamaica tell an alternate story. Once known as the "Wickedest City on The planet," Port Illustrious was a famous privateer safe house during the seventeenth hundred years. The city met a disastrous destiny in 1692 when a strong seismic tremor sent a critical part of it into the ocean.

The submerged unearthings of Port Illustrious have uncovered a lively center point of oceanic movement frozen in time. Very much protected structures, wrecks, and curios offer a brief look into the privateer culture that once flourished inside its walls. The depressed city of Port Regal fills in as an unmistakable connection to a turbulent time of sea history, where privateers, privateers, and brokers united in a dynamic and uncivilized climate.

Daring toward the northeastern shore of Egypt, the lowered city of Thonis-Heracleion rises out of the profundities of Aboukir Sound. Known as Heracleion to the old Greeks and Thonis to the Egyptians, this once-prosperous city filled in as a flourishing port during the hour of the pharaohs. Thonis-Heracleion's submersion, accepted to have happened in the eighth century BC, consigned it to the domain of fantasy and legend for a really long time.

The submerged vestiges of Thonis-Heracleion, found in the mid 21st 100 years, recount an account of magnificence and social trade. As jumpers investigate the lowered city, they reveal gigantic sculptures, unpredictably cut stelae, and the remainders of a fantastic sanctuary

committed to the goddess Isis. The city's very much arranged metropolitan design, complete with trenches and harbors, gives important bits of knowledge into the oceanic associations and social impacts of old Egypt.

One of the most striking finds in Thonis-Heracleion was the disclosure of a submerged boat stacked with treasures. The boat's freight, including gold coins, gems, and strict contributions, offers a substantial association with the city's lively sea exchange. Thonis-Heracleion's submersion has been credited to a mix of catastrophic events, including seismic tremors and rising ocean levels, featuring the weakness of even the most prosperous urban communities to the powers of nature.

Venturing toward the western shoreline of India, the lowered city of Dwarka coaxes wayfarers and archeologists. As indicated by Hindu folklore, Dwarka was the incredible realm of Master Krishna, a heavenly city accepted to have been established a while back. While Dwarka's presence was for some time consigned to the domain of folklore, submerged investigations off the shore of Gujarat have uncovered unquestionable proof of a once-flourishing old city.

The submerged vestiges of Dwarka, found in the late twentieth hundred years, line up with portrayals of the legendary city tracked down in old texts like the Mahabharata and the Puranas. The lowered designs, including walls, support points, and ancient rarities, relate to the perplexing city arranging credited to Ruler Krishna's realm. The disclosure of Dwarka brings up issues about the verifiable premise of old legends and the likely convergences among folklore and archaic exploration.

The appeal of examining archeological disclosures reaches out past old urban communities to wartime wrecks, offering bits of knowledge into the human expense of contention and the innovations of war. In the frigid waters of the Cold, the remaining parts of Franklin's lost undertaking lie covered in secret. Sir John Franklin, an English wayfarer, set forth in 1845 with two ships, the HMS Erebus and the HMS Fear, looking for the Northwest Entry.

The Cold, with its misleading ice and brutal circumstances, demonstrated unforgiving. The destiny of Franklin's undertaking became quite possibly of the best secret in sea history. For quite a long time, the whereabouts of the two boats and the destiny of the team stayed obscure, powering hypothesis and investigation. In 2014 and 2016, the disaster areas of both the HMS Erebus and the HMS Dread were found underneath the cold waters of the Canadian Icy.

The astoundingly all around protected condition of the boats, alongside the antiquities found inside, offered bits of knowledge into the difficulties looked by Franklin and his team. The chilly, dull profundities of the Icy Sea had defended the remaining parts of the campaign, safeguarding a sad section in the mission for oceanic investigation. The revelation of Franklin's lost campaign features the double idea of submerged investigation — revealing the victories and misfortunes of human undertakings.

In the Pacific Sea, the destruction of the USS Indianapolis lays on the sea floor, a solemn demonstration of the human expense of war. The USS Indianapolis, a Portland-class weighty cruiser, assumed a vital part in The Second Great War, conveying parts of the nuclear bomb that would later be dropped on Hiroshima. In the wake of finishing this mysterious mission, the boat was obliterated by a Japanese submarine on July 30, 1945, sinking quickly.

The team confronted impossible abhorrences as they anticipated salvage in shark-pervaded waters. The sinking of the USS Indianapolis brought about one of the best oceanic calamities in U.S. history, with just a negligible portion of the team enduring the difficulty. The specific area of the destruction stayed obscure for a really long time, adding to the secret encompassing the destiny of the boat and its team. In 2017, the destruction of the USS Indianapolis was found in the Philippine Ocean by a group drove by Microsoft prime supporter Paul Allen.

The submerged undertaking found the tragically missing boat as well as given conclusion to the groups of the individuals who had died. The revelation brought the disastrous story of the USS Indianapolis back into the public awareness, helping the world to remember the penances made during wartime. The lowered remaining parts of the USS Indianapolis act as an impactful commemoration to the ones who served on board the boat and the difficulties looked by the individuals who explore the risky waters of war.

While the investigation of archeological revelations uncovers the secrets of the past, it likewise raises moral contemplations and difficulties. The fragile harmony between logical request and the safeguarding of submerged social legacy is a subject of progressing banter inside the archeological local area. The submerged locales, whether old urban communities or wartime wrecks, are vulnerable to natural dangers, plundering, and accidental harm from human exercises.

Safeguarding these lowered fortunes requires a multidisciplinary approach that joins archeological mastery, mechanical development, and ecological stewardship. Propels in submerged mechanical technology, remote detecting advances, and painless overview techniques have empowered scientists to investigate and archive lowered destinations without truly hurting delicate conditions. The fragile dance among investigation and protection is fundamental to guarantee that these submerged marvels stay in one piece for people in the future.

The examination of archeological disclosures stretches out past Earth, venturing into the domains of extraterrestrial investigation. On one of Jupiter's moons, Europa, researchers estimate about the chance of a subsurface sea underneath its frosty hull. The potential for fluid water on Europa brings up tempting issues about the possibility of extraterrestrial life.

While Europa's sea stays stowed away from direct perception, researchers assemble hints from the moon's surface highlights, including breaks, edges, and tumultuous landscape. These elements recommend the powerful interchange between the cold covering and the subsurface sea underneath. The investigation of Europa's subsurface sea addresses another wilderness in astrobiology, as researchers contemplate the possible livability of this far off moon.

The equals between Earth's seas and Europa's subsurface sea welcome hypothesis about the potential for life past our planet. In the event that Europa harbors life, it would reclassify how we might interpret the circumstances vital for science to arise. The mission to investigate the profundities of Europa's sea includes planning complex space tests and instruments fit for entering its frosty outside layer to look for indications of something going on under the surface in obscurity, bone chilling profundities.

As mankind examines the secrets of archeological revelations and the potential for extraterrestrial seas, the association among investigation and the human soul becomes obvious. The bait of the obscure, whether concealed inside the World's seas or in the frosty scopes of far off moons, coaxes pilgrims to push the limits of information and understanding.

Archeological disclosures, whether ashore or underneath the waves, act as windows into the past, offering unmistakable associations with the civilizations that molded our reality. The examination of these revelations is a demonstration of human interest, versatility, and the quest for information. From the lowered urban communities of Pompeii and Thonis-Heracleion to the submerged boats of Franklin's endeavor and the USS Indianapolis, every revelation adds a layer to the rich embroidery of mankind's set of experiences.

In the profundities of the sea, where daylight blurs and quiet rules, the leftovers of past civilizations and the mysteries they hold keep on calling. As we investigate, unearth, and decipher the follows left by the individuals who preceded us, we set out on an excursion that rises above time, interfacing the present to the consistently unfurling story of humankind. The examination of archeological disclosures isn't just a scholarly pursuit; it is a significant investigation of our common legacy, a journey to comprehend where we come from and, likewise, where we may be going.

3.3 Speculation on the reasons for the submersion of these once-thriving societies.

Hypothesis on the purposes behind the submersion of once-flourishing social orders is a complex undertaking that interweaves topographical, natural, and anthropological elements. The lowered urban communities, going from the old asphalts of Pavlopetri to the privateer swarmed roads of Port Illustrious, share a typical destiny — they capitulated to the determined powers of nature, either through devastating occasions or progressive changes in ecological circumstances.

Pavlopetri, settled off the southern shore of Laconia in Greece, ended up lowered, not because of the activities of an attacking power or cultural breakdown, yet rather as an outcome of seismic action and geographical cycles. The district is inclined to quakes, and the city's submersion around 1000 BCE is credited to a mix of tremors and the slow sinking of the land. This geographical precariousness changed the geology, making Pavlopetri progressively slip underneath the waves, where it stayed concealed for centuries.

Conversely, the destiny of Port Imperial, once famous as the "Wickedest City on The planet," was fixed in 1692 by a strong tremor. Situated off the shoreline of Jamaica, Port Regal was a clamoring center of exchange, robbery, and lewdness during the seventeenth 100 years. The tremor that struck on June 7, 1692, brought about a huge part

MYSTERIES OF THE DEEP BLUE

of the city sliding into the ocean. The unexpected submersion of Port Regal was a result of both the seismic action and the city's problematic area on low-lying, temperamental ground.

Thonis-Heracleion, an old city at the mouth of the Nile, confronted an alternate destiny. Lowered around the eighth century BCE, the city's downfall is credited to a blend of geographical and anthropogenic elements. Rising ocean levels, subsidence of the land, and the intensifying impacts of seismic tremors added to the continuous submersion of Thonis-Heracleion. Also, the changing direction of the Nile Stream and the gathering of silt additionally modified the scene, rushing the city's plummet into the profundities.

Dwarka, the amazing city of Ruler Krishna off the bank of Gujarat, India, is wrapped in fantasy and history. The submersion of Dwarka, accepted to have happened around 1500 BCE, brings up issues about the exchange among normal and social powers. Topographical variables, for example, seismic movement or changes in ocean level, could play had an impact in Dwarka's submersion. Nonetheless, the legendary stories recommend an association between the city's downfall and a help from above — a component that adds layers of intricacy to the hypothesis encompassing its submersion.

The investigation of Franklin's lost campaign in the Cold uncovers an alternate feature of submersion — one impacted by the super polar climate. Sir John Franklin's mission for the Northwest Section in 1845 finished in misfortune as both the HMS Erebus and the HMS Dread capitulated to the ice-shrouded waters. The cruel Icy circumstances, including ocean ice and frigid temperatures, established a hazardous climate for the campaign. Ice ensnarement, joined with the groups' battles against the components, prompted the possible submersion of the boats, which stayed concealed until their revelation in 2014 and 2016.

The USS Indianapolis, a weighty cruiser that assumed an essential part in The Second Great War, met an alternate destiny in the Pacific Sea. Obliterated by a Japanese submarine on July 30, 1945, the boat sank quickly, leaving the team abandoned in shark-swarmed waters.

| 71 |

The awfulness of the USS Indianapolis was not an aftereffect of topographical cycles yet rather an outcome of wartime activities. The sinking, intensified by the absence of a pain call and postponed salvage endeavors, brought about perhaps of the main maritime debacle ever.

As the examination of these lowered locales unfurls, the purposes behind their submersion become woven into a story that stretches out past the land and ecological aspects. The destiny of these once-flourishing social orders mirrors the sensitive harmony between human undertakings and the unique powers of the regular world. While geographical cycles, quakes, and moving scenes assumed critical parts at times, human exercises, whether through fighting, investigation, or cultural decisions, additionally added to the submersion of these civilizations.

On account of old urban communities like Pavlopetri and Thonis-Heracleion, the interaction of regular and anthropogenic variables is clear. The land weaknesses of the areas, combined with the decisions by the occupants, affected the urban communities' fates. Port Imperial's submersion, then again, is a distinct sign of how human exercises related to land insecurity can prompt the unexpected death of a flourishing city.

The legend touched submersion of Dwarka adds a layer of intricacy, entwining social stories with expected topographical and ecological elements. The incredible stories of Ruler Krishna's realm being gulped by the ocean bring out a feeling of help from above, mixing the domains of folklore and verifiable request. Unwinding the explanations behind Dwarka's submersion requires exploring the convergence of strict convictions and logical investigation.

In the Icy, the submersion of Franklin's undertaking and its very much saved wrecks offer bits of knowledge into the difficulties presented by outrageous conditions. The Icy's frosty grasp, portrayed via ocean ice, cold temperatures, and seclusion, transformed an aggressive journey for investigation into a grievous story of endurance and misfortune. The submerged remainders of Franklin's boats act as both a verifiable record and a demonstration of the unforgiving idea of polar investigation.

The USS Indianapolis, a loss from war, addresses the human cost extricated by struggle. The sinking of the cruiser, obliterated in the last long periods of The Second Great War, remains as a grave sign of the penances made chasing international objectives. The submerged destruction, found many years after the fact, fills in as an unmistakable remembrance to the group and the difficulties they looked in the immense scopes of the Pacific Sea.

Past the natural domains, the hypothesis on the submersion of once-flourishing social orders reaches out to the potential for extraterrestrial seas. On Jupiter's moon, Europa, the hypothesis spins around the presence of a subsurface sea underneath its cold outside layer. The secrets of Europa's sea, stowed away from direct perception, flash interest in the circumstances important for life past Earth.

Assuming Europa's subsurface sea harbors life, it would reclassify how we might interpret tenability in the universe. The journey to investigate this outsider sea includes planning shuttle fit for entering the moon's frigid outside. The equals between Earth's seas and the expected expanses of Europa fuel the hypothesis that the fundamental elements for life might reach out past our home planet.

Hypothesis on the explanations behind the submersion of these once-flourishing social orders interlaces logical request with a profound appreciation for the intricacies of mankind's set of experiences and the regular world. From seismic movements and land cycles to the effects of war and investigation, each lowered site recounts a one of a kind story of wins, misfortunes, and the persevering through flexibility of the human soul.

As the investigation of these lowered urban areas and wrecks proceeds, the multidisciplinary idea of archeological examination turns out to be progressively clear. Geologists, archeologists, history specialists, and researchers from different fields team up to unwind the secrets of the past. The speculative excursion into the explanations behind submersion is a demonstration of the human limit with respect to interest, investigation, and the quest for information across both natural and extraterrestrial scenes.

In the terrific embroidered artwork of history, the lowered urban communities and wrecks stand as strong tokens of the fleetingness of human accomplishments and the powerful exchange among civic establishments and the regular powers that shape our planet. The continuous investigation of these lowered locales holds the commitment of additional disclosures, testing how we might interpret the past and offering new viewpoints on the complicated dance between human social orders and the always changing scenes they occupy.

Chapter 4

"The Bermuda Triangle: Fact or Fiction?"

The Bermuda Triangle, a locale in the western piece of the North Atlantic Sea, has for some time been covered in secret and hypothesis. Frequently alluded to as "Satan's Triangle," this region has gained notoriety for purportedly being the site of various unexplained vanishings of boats and airplane. While some put stock in the heavenly clarifications encompassing the Bermuda Triangle, others contend that there is a logical reason for the revealed episodes. In this investigation of the Bermuda Triangle, we will dig into the set of experiences, hypotheses, and proof encompassing this perplexing district to decide if the secrets are truth or fiction.

The historical backdrop of the Bermuda Triangle's strange standing can be followed back to the mid-twentieth century when the term was first authored. The expression acquired boundless fame after a progression of articles composed by writer Vincent Gaddis during the 1960s. Gaddis' articles and ensuing books portrayed a locale where ships and planes apparently evaporated suddenly, abandoning just inquiries and hypothesis.

One of the earliest and most well known episodes frequently connected with the Bermuda Triangle is the vanishing of Flight 19 in December 1945. Flight 19 was a unit of five U.S. Naval force planes on a preparation mission. The planes, drove by experienced pilot Lieutenant Charles Taylor, became muddled and in the end ran out of fuel. Notwithstanding broad inquiry endeavors, neither the airplane nor the 14 team individuals were at any point found. This occurrence, alongside others, filled the persona encompassing the Bermuda Triangle.

Nonetheless, it's crucial for note that the Bermuda Triangle is definitely not a formally acknowledged geographic area. The term isn't utilized by the U.S. government or any global sea association. As a matter of fact, the limits of the Bermuda Triangle are not generally settled upon, and various sources give various meanings of its area. A few sources characterize it as a three-sided region with vertices in Miami, Bermuda, and Puerto Rico, while others have various directions for its limits.

As hypotheses and hypothesis about the Bermuda Triangle multiplied, specialists and researchers started to analyze the supposed peculiarities related with the area. One conspicuous logical clarification centers around the presence of methane hydrates in the sea floor. Methane hydrates are ice-like designs containing methane gas that can be found in specific seabed dregs. The hypothesis recommends that huge arrivals of methane gas from the sea floor could make shakiness in the water, prompting abrupt and rough emissions. These emissions, thusly, could upset the lightness of boats, making them sink quickly suddenly.

While this methane hydrate hypothesis offers a conceivable logical clarification for a portion of the revealed vanishings, it doesn't represent the vanishings of airplane. Also, there is restricted proof to help the possibility that methane hydrate ejections are normal or strong enough to cause the size of occurrences credited to the Bermuda Triangle.

Another logical viewpoint centers around the job of attractive peculiarities nearby. The Bermuda Triangle is one of the puts on Earth where genuine north and attractive north adjust. This arrangement can prompt compass readings that are less precise than in different districts.

Assuming that pilots or guides neglect to represent this inconsistency, they could err their situation and course, possibly prompting navigational mistakes and episodes.

Notwithstanding regular clarifications, human mistake and ecological elements assume critical parts in oceanic and aeronautics episodes. The sea is tremendous and can be tricky, with eccentric atmospheric conditions, solid flows, and unexpected tempests. Pilots and mariners, even with trend setting innovation, can experience provokes that lead to mishaps and vanishings.

Besides, the verifiable record of episodes in the Bermuda Triangle has been raised doubt about. A large number of the tales related with the district have been sensationalized or erroneously detailed.

Now and again, examinations have uncovered that the strange vanishings had coherent and non-baffling clarifications. For instance, destruction from probably evaporated planes and ships has been found, and in certain examples, human blunder, mechanical disappointment, or unfriendly weather still up in the air to be the reason.

Regardless of the logical and objective clarifications offered, the charm of the Bermuda Triangle as a wellspring of paranormal movement perseveres in mainstream society. Books, narratives, and films keep on sustaining the fantasy, frequently stressing the otherworldly angles and making light of or disregarding the logical proof. The possibility of a secretive and perilous district where the laws of physical science and nature appear to separate catches the creative mind and feeds into the human interest with the unexplored world.

As of late, headways in innovation have permitted researchers to investigate the sea floor to a greater extent and assemble information that was beforehand out of reach. Remote detecting gadgets, submerged vehicles, and further developed planning strategies have given specialists a superior comprehension of the geography and geology of the sea depths in the Bermuda Triangle district.

One prominent disclosure is the presence of huge holes on the sea floor that were logical shaped by methane hydrate blasts. While these cavities recommend that such blasts can happen, they don't be guaranteed to affirm that the Bermuda Triangle is an especially dangerous region. Comparable arrangements have been found in different regions of the planet, showing that methane hydrate blasts are not exceptional to this district.

The absence of convincing proof supporting the otherworldly hypotheses related with the Bermuda Triangle has driven numerous researchers and cynics to excuse the whole idea as a fantasy. Nonetheless, the appeal of the obscure and the human propensity to look for clarifications for baffling occasions keep on filling faith in the paranormal parts of the Bermuda Triangle.

In the domain of flying, innovation plays had a critical impact in further developing wellbeing and forestalling mishaps. Current airplane are furnished with complex route frameworks, specialized gadgets, and wellbeing highlights that make them stronger to unexpected difficulties. Additionally, headways in weather conditions anticipating and correspondence have improved the capacity of pilots to explore securely through testing conditions.

Sea wellbeing has likewise seen huge enhancements with the improvement of cutting edge route frameworks, satellite correspondence, and search and salvage capacities. The Worldwide Oceanic Association (IMO) and other administrative bodies have executed severe security guidelines and conventions to guarantee the prosperity of sailors and the security of sea transportation.

As how we might interpret the World's seas and environment extends, the once-puzzling parts of the Bermuda Triangle are steadily being demystified. While the locale might present moves for route because of attractive inconsistencies and regular peculiarities, there is no logical reason for the powerful clarifications that have been ascribed to it.

All in all, the Bermuda Triangle stays a charming and enamoring subject that has caught the public's creative mind for a really long time. While the secrets related with this area have been exposed by logical examination, the charm of the obscure and the longing for otherworldly clarifications keep on sustaining the legend. It is fundamental for people to move toward the subject with a basic mentality, taking into account the logical proof and reasonable clarifications that shed light on the real essence of the Bermuda Triangle. At last, isolating truth from fiction permits us to see the value in the intricacies of the normal world without surrendering to the enticement of sentimentality and unwarranted hypothesis.

4.1 Analysis of the myths and legends surrounding the Bermuda Triangle.

The fantasies and legends encompassing the Bermuda Triangle have dazzled the human creative mind for a really long time, adding to the persona and air of this puzzling district in the western piece of the North Atlantic Sea. While the expression "Bermuda Triangle" isn't formally acknowledged by any worldwide sea association, the tales and hypothesis related with this area have led to a plenty of legends, frequently mixing truth with fiction.

One pervasive legend includes the possibility that the Bermuda Triangle is where ordinary laws of physical science and nature stop applying. As per this legend, the district is a passage to one more aspect or an entry through which boats and airplane can strangely disappear. This powerful story has been propagated in books, motion pictures, and TV programs, adding to the famous picture of the Bermuda Triangle as a zone of puzzling peculiarities.

The charm of such mysterious accounts lies in the human interest with the obscure and the craving to make sense of apparently unexplainable occasions. In any case, according to a logical point of view, there is no proof to help the thought that the Bermuda Triangle opposes the laws of material science or works outside the domain of regular powers. While the locale might present navigational difficulties, crediting extraordinary characteristics to it misses the mark on establishment in experimental perception and logical examination.

One more getting through legend related with the Bermuda Triangle is the possibility that it is a hotbed of extraterrestrial action.

A few defenders of this hypothesis propose that outsider creatures or unidentified flying items (UFOs) are liable for the vanishings of boats and airplane in the district. While reports of UFO sightings have been recorded, the association between these sightings and the implied vanishings needs decisive proof.

The extraterrestrial hypothesis frequently depends on episodic records and unsubstantiated observer declaration, making it hard to lay out a causal connection among UFOs and the supposed occurrences in the Bermuda Triangle. In addition, established researchers accentuates the requirement for thorough experimental proof and certain information to help any cases of extraterrestrial association. At this point, the possibility that outsiders are liable for the secrets of the Bermuda Triangle remains solidly dug in the domain of hypothesis and sci-fi.

One of the most renowned legends connected to the Bermuda Triangle is the account of the lost city of Atlantis. As indicated by this legend, the leftovers of the antiquated and high level civilization of Atlantis lie concealed underneath the waters of the Bermuda Triangle. Defenders of this hypothesis highlight claimed submerged structures, oddities on sonar readings, and puzzling developments as proof of a lowered city.

While the legend of Atlantis has caught the human creative mind for a really long time, standard prehistoric studies and topography don't uphold the possibility of a depressed city in the Bermuda Triangle. The logical agreement is that Atlantis, assuming it at any point existed, is bound to be tracked down in the Mediterranean area, as portrayed in the works of the antiquated Greek rationalist Plato. The relationship between the Bermuda Triangle and Atlantis fills in to act as an illustration of how fantasies and fables can become entwined, making stories that catch the public's creative mind in spite of an absence of exact proof.

Ocean beasts and legendary animals likewise track down a spot in the embroidery of Bermuda Triangle fantasies. A few stories depict experiences with monster ocean snakes, legendary monsters, or supernatural animals that are said to occupy the waters of the district. These stories, frequently went down through ages, add a component of imagination to the secret of the Bermuda Triangle.

From a logical viewpoint, the presence of ocean beasts or legendary animals in the Bermuda Triangle isn't upheld by dependable proof. A large number of these accounts need evident sources and depend on emotionalism as opposed to experimental perception. The human inclination to wind around fantastical stories around unexplained occasions can add to the propagation of such legends, further clouding the line among reality and fiction.

One of the persevering through secrets of the Bermuda Triangle is the vanishing of Flight 19 in December 1945. This occurrence included five U.S. Naval force planes on a standard preparation mission, drove by Lieutenant Charles Taylor. The planes became confused, ran out of fuel, and were gone forever. The vanishing of Flight 19 has been refered to as one of the key occasions that added to the persona of the Bermuda Triangle.

While the tale of Flight 19 is a verifiable reality, the legend encompassing it has developed throughout the long term, for certain records decorating subtleties and presenting powerful components.

The logical examination concerning the vanishing of Flight 19 focuses to navigational mistakes, unfavorable weather patterns, and fuel fatigue as likely explanations. The episode fills in as a sign of this present reality challenges that pilots and guides can confront, particularly in regions with attractive peculiarities and eccentric weather conditions.

Another notable occurrence related with the Bermuda Triangle is the vanishing of the SS Cyclops in Walk 1918. The SS Cyclops was a U.S. Naval force freight transport that disappeared suddenly, alongside its team of 309 individuals. The conditions encompassing the vanishing of the SS Cyclops stay a subject of hypothesis and discussion.

While the deficiency of the SS Cyclops is a verifiable occasion, different speculations have arisen to make sense of its vanishing. Some recommend that the boat succumbed to a German submarine during The Second Great War, while others suggest that it was surpassed by an unexpected and devastating occasion, like an underlying disappointment or outrageous weather patterns. In spite of broad pursuit endeavors, the destruction of the SS Cyclops has never been found, adding to the persevering through secret of its vanishing.

The Bermuda Triangle has likewise been connected to the vanishing of the USS Cyclops, a Naval force freight transport that evaporated without a follow in Walk 1918. While the deficiency of the USS Cyclops is a verifiable truth, different hypotheses have arisen to make sense of its vanishing. Some recommend that the boat succumbed to a German submarine during The Second Great War, while others suggest that it was overwhelmed by an unexpected and horrendous occasion, like a primary disappointment or outrageous weather patterns. Notwithstanding broad hunt endeavors, the destruction of the USS Cyclops has never been found, adding to the getting through secret of its vanishing.

The Bermuda Triangle has likewise been related with the baffling instance of the Mary Celeste, a dealer transport found loose and deserted in the Atlantic Sea in 1872. While the Mary Celeste is much of the time refered to act as an illustration of a vessel that disappeared suddenly, the genuine conditions encompassing its relinquishment are more nuanced.

The Mary Celeste was found by the group of another boat, the Dei Gratia, which ran over the vessel floating off the Azores. The boat was generally unblemished, with indications of a rushed takeoff, like to some extent spread out sails and a missing raft. In any case, the freight and individual effects of the group were to a great extent undisturbed. The destiny of the team of the Mary Celeste stays obscure, and different hypotheses have been proposed, including the chance of a navigational mistake, robbery, or unfairness. The episode, while secretive, isn't elite to the Bermuda Triangle and is frequently refered to show the vulnerabilities and risks looked via sailors in the nineteenth 100 years.

In analyzing the fantasies and legends encompassing the Bermuda Triangle, obviously the line among reality and fiction is frequently obscured. The charm of the obscure, combined with the human propensity to look for clarifications for unexplained occasions, has led to an intricate embroidery of stories that reach from the conceivable to the fantastical.

According to a logical point of view, a considerable lot of the fantasies and legends need sound proof and depend on recounted records, drama, or misinterpretations of verifiable occasions. The test lies in recognizing undeniable realities and the embellishments that have gathered throughout the long term through narrating and mainstream society.

The Bermuda Triangle, as an idea, fills in as a wake up call about the effect of fantasies and legends on open discernment. The district's standing has been molded by authentic occasions as well as by the inventive accounts that have been woven around them. As we unwind the strings of these legends, it is crucial for approach the subject with a basic outlook and an appreciation for the intricacies of history, science, and human narrating.

All in all, the fantasies and legends encompassing the Bermuda Triangle uncover the complicated transaction among the real world and creative mind. While the district has seen truly authentic occasions that keep on confusing analysts, the embellishments and heavenly components woven into its story feature the persevering through human interest with secret and the unexplained. As we explore the waters of legend and reality, it is vital to move toward the Bermuda Triangle with an insightful eye, isolating the unmistakable proof from the speculative stories that have filled its persona for ages.

4.2 Examination of real-life disappearances and mysterious phenomena in the region.

The Bermuda Triangle, a locale in the western piece of the North Atlantic Sea, has gained notoriety for puzzling vanishings and unexplained peculiarities. While a considerable lot of the detailed occurrences have been exposed or credited to normal causes, there are cases where the secrets stay inexplicable, adding to the persevering through persona of the area. This assessment digs into genuine vanishings and secretive peculiarities in the Bermuda Triangle, investigating current realities and hypotheses encompassing these occasions.

Quite possibly of the earliest kept vanishing in the Bermuda Triangle is that of Flight 19 in December 1945. This episode included five U.S. Naval force planes on a normal preparation mission. The unit, drove by experienced pilot Lieutenant Charles Taylor, became perplexed over the Atlantic and in the long run ran out of fuel. In spite of broad hunt endeavors, neither the planes nor the 14 team individuals were at any point found.

The vanishing of Flight 19 has been the subject of much hypothesis and investigation. While some have credited the episode to powerful or extraterrestrial causes, the authority examination highlighted a mix of navigational blunders, horrible weather patterns, and miscommunications. The region's attractive inconsistencies, which can influence compass readings, were likewise thought to be as potential variables prompting the confusion of the group.

Regardless of the broad inquiry and resulting examinations, the destruction of Flight 19 has never been found, adding a component of secret to the episode. The vanishing of these airplanes and their group individuals stays one of the persevering through puzzles related with the Bermuda Triangle, with discusses going on about the exact elements that prompted their disappearing.

In Walk 1918, one more prominent vanishing happened with the USS Cyclops, a U.S. Naval force freight transport. The vessel, with a group of 309 individuals, evaporated without a follow while on the way from Barbados to Baltimore. The vanishing of the USS Cyclops is viewed as one of the best oceanic secrets in U.S. history.

Different speculations have been proposed to make sense of the destiny of the USS Cyclops. Some recommend that the boat succumbed to a German submarine during The Second Great War, while others highlight the chance of underlying disappointment due to overburdening or outrageous weather patterns. In spite of broad pursuit endeavors, including the arrangement of maritime vessels and airplane, no destruction or flotsam and jetsam from the USS Cyclops was at any point found.

MYSTERIES OF THE DEEP BLUE

The secret encompassing the USS Cyclops developed with the absence of a pain call or any difficult situation before its vanishing. The case stays inexplicable, and the destiny of the boat and its group is one of the getting through puzzles related with the Bermuda Triangle.

The SS El Faro, a freight transport, turned into the focal point of consideration in October 2015 when it vanished nearby the Bermuda Triangle during Storm Joaquin. The boat, with a team of 33, was in transit from Jacksonville, Florida, to San Juan, Puerto Rico. The U.S. Coast Watchman led a broad hunt, finding garbage and the boat's destruction around three miles beneath the outer layer of the Atlantic Sea.

The examination concerning the SS El Faro's vanishing uncovered that the boat had cruised straightforwardly into the way of Typhoon Joaquin, a Classification 4 tempest at that point. The vessel's age and primary issues were likewise distinguished as contributing elements to its sinking. The episode featured the risks presented by strong tempests in the vast ocean and the significance of reasonable route and navigation.

While the SS El Faro's vanishing was terrible, the examination didn't yield proof of any secretive or paranormal causes. The episode highlighted this present reality challenges that oceanic vessels face, especially while exploring through deceptive weather patterns.

Notwithstanding vanishings, the Bermuda Triangle has been related with episodes including electronic glitches and correspondence disappointments. A few reports propose that boats and airplane entering the locale experience irregularities in their navigational hardware, compasses, and correspondence frameworks. These electronic glitches are frequently refered to as proof of the baffling powers at play in the Bermuda Triangle.

Nonetheless, from a logical stance, electronic breakdowns can be credited to various variables, including normal peculiarities, gear disappointment, or human mistake. Attractive abnormalities nearby, which can influence compass readings, are one conceivable clarification for navigational issues. The mind boggling communications between electromagnetic fields and the World's geomagnetic highlights might prompt disturbances in electronic hardware, however such peculiarities are not novel to the Bermuda Triangle.

One episode that acquired consideration for its accounted for electronic breakdowns is the situation of the USS Nimitz UFO experience in 2004. This occurrence included experiences with unidentified airborne peculiarities (UAP) by U.S. Naval force pilots off the shoreline of California, not inside the Bermuda Triangle. While the episode has been generally examined with regards to UFOs and military experiences, it fills in to act as an illustration of how reports of electronic oddities can be related with a scope of conditions and areas, not restricted to the Bermuda Triangle.

The Bermuda Triangle has additionally been connected to reports of attractive inconsistencies that could influence route and correspondence frameworks. The locale is known for errors between obvious north and attractive north, prompting varieties in compass readings. Be that as it may, these varieties are indisputable and don't be guaranteed to represent an exceptional danger to route.

While attractive irregularities can add to navigational difficulties, particularly for the people who neglect to represent the distinctions among valid and attractive north, established researchers accentuates that such inconsistencies are not select to the Bermuda Triangle. Comparative varieties in attractive fields can be tracked down in different regions of the planet, and navigational outlines are consistently refreshed to give exact data to mariners and pilots.

The secret encompassing the Bermuda Triangle has likewise been powered by the revelation of submerged developments and designs that some have proposed are proof of antiquated human advancements or extraterrestrial movement. Sonar readings and submerged planning have uncovered uncommon highlights on the sea depths, like huge holes and developments, starting hypothesis about their beginnings.

One outstanding revelation is the supposed Bimini Street, a progression of lowered limestone closes off the bank of Bimini in the Bahamas.

A few defenders guarantee that these developments are the leftovers of an old and high level progress, conceivably Atlantis. In any case, standard archeologists and geologists characteristic the Bimini Street to regular land processes, for example, beachrock development, and excuse the possibility of an old civilization nearby.

Also, enormous holes on the sea depths, frequently connected with methane hydrate emissions, have been found in the Bermuda Triangle district. While these pits give experiences into topographical cycles, they don't uphold the thought of a puzzling or heavenly clarification for the district's secrets. Methane hydrate ejections, while charming, are not one of a kind to the Bermuda Triangle and happen in different regions of the planet.

The investigation of submerged highlights has contributed significant information to how we might interpret the World's geography, yet the jump from logical perception to powerful translation requires alert. The propensity to credit unexplained peculiarities to antiquated developments or extraterrestrial movement can eclipse the regular cycles that shape the World's surface.

The Bermuda Triangle's relationship with strange vanishings and peculiarities has prompted different hypotheses and clarifications, going from logical to speculative. One predominant logical clarification centers around the presence of methane hydrates in the sea depths. Methane hydrates are ice-like designs containing methane gas that can be found in specific seabed silt.

The hypothesis proposes that enormous arrivals of methane gas from the sea floor could make shakiness in the water, prompting abrupt and vicious ejections. These emissions, thusly, could upset the lightness of boats, making them sink quickly suddenly. While this methane hydrate hypothesis offers a conceivable logical clarification for a portion of the revealed vanishings, it doesn't represent the vanishings of airplane and has restricted observational proof to help its broad event in the Bermuda Triangle.

Another logical point of view centers around attractive abnormalities nearby. The Bermuda Triangle is one of the puts on Earth where genuine north and attractive north adjust. This arrangement can prompt compass readings that are less exact than in different locales. Assuming that pilots or guides neglect to represent this disparity, they could miscount their situation and course, possibly prompting navigational blunders and episodes.

Notwithstanding normal clarifications, human mistake and natural elements assume huge parts in sea and aeronautics episodes. The sea is huge and can be slippery, with capricious atmospheric conditions, solid flows, and unexpected tempests. Pilots and mariners, even with cutting edge innovation, can experience provokes that lead to mishaps and vanishings.

The assessment of genuine vanishings and puzzling peculiarities in the Bermuda Triangle highlights the intricacy of the locale's standing. While certain occurrences stay perplexing and add to the getting through persona of the area, others have been made sense of through logical request and judicious investigation. The appeal of the obscure and the longing for thrilling clarifications keep on molding public view of the Bermuda Triangle, emphasiz.

4.3 Scientific explanations for the occurrences and dispelling common misconceptions.

The Bermuda Triangle, frequently covered in secret and hypothesis, has been a subject of interest and legend for a really long time. While various hypotheses and legends encompass this locale, researchers and scientists have looked to give objective and proof based clarifications for the events ascribed to the Bermuda Triangle. This investigation means to dig into the logical clarifications for the occurrences and dissipate normal misguided judgments related with this confounding region in the western piece of the North Atlantic Sea.

One of the conspicuous logical points of view centers around the job of attractive oddities in the Bermuda Triangle. The World's attractive field isn't uniform, and certain regions, including the Bermuda

Triangle, display varieties in attractive force. This variety brings about errors between obvious north (geographic north) and attractive north (the course a compass focuses), prompting what is known as attractive declination.

Navigational instruments, like compasses, depend on exact readings of attractive north to decide heading. In areas with critical attractive irregularities, guides might encounter difficulties in getting exact compass readings. Assuming pilots or mariners neglect to change their route frameworks for attractive declination, it can bring about navigational blunders, possibly prompting confusion and occurrences.

While attractive peculiarities in the Bermuda Triangle are genuine, it's pivotal to underline that they are not remarkable to this locale. Comparative varieties exist in different regions of the planet, and navigational graphs are consistently refreshed to give precise data to pilots and mariners. The logical comprehension of attractive oddities exposes the misinterpretation that the Bermuda Triangle has powerful or secretive attractive powers that disturb route in phenomenal ways.

Another logical clarification centers around the presence of methane hydrates in the sea floor. Methane hydrates are ice-like designs containing methane gas that structure under unambiguous circumstances.

The hypothesis proposes that enormous arrivals of methane from the sea floor could make flimsiness in the water, bringing about unexpected and fierce emissions. These emissions could disturb the lightness of boats, making them sink quickly suddenly.

While the methane hydrate hypothesis offers a conceivable logical clarification for a portion of the revealed vanishings, it has restrictions. As a matter of some importance, there is restricted experimental proof to recommend that monstrous arrivals of methane hydrates happen much of the time in the Bermuda Triangle. Also, the hypothesis fundamentally addresses sea episodes and doesn't completely represent the vanishings of airplane in the district.

Besides, research has uncovered that huge pits on the sea floor, frequently connected with methane hydrate blasts, exist in different regions of the planet too. This difficulties that the Bermuda Triangle is remarkably inclined to such land peculiarities. While methane hydrates are charming, crediting far reaching vanishings exclusively to their emissions misrepresents the mind boggling connections of normal powers in the World's seas.

Meteorological factors likewise assume a vital part in figuring out episodes inside the Bermuda Triangle. The area is known for its eccentric atmospheric conditions, including unexpected and extreme tempests. Such climate occasions can present huge difficulties for pilots and mariners, prompting mishaps and vanishings. Solid breezes, fierce oceans, and fast changes in barometrical strain can make unsafe circumstances, particularly for more modest vessels and airplane.

The verifiable record of occurrences in the Bermuda Triangle frequently uncovers a connection between's accounted for vanishings and unfavorable weather patterns. Unexpected and fierce tempests can overpower vessels, undermining their underlying uprightness and delivering them defenseless against sinking. On account of airplane, extreme disturbance and unfriendly weather conditions can add to crashes.

An illustrative model is the vanishing of Flight 19 in December 1945. The group of U.S. Naval force planes, drove by Lieutenant Charles Taylor, experienced unfavorable weather patterns during a standard preparation mission. The blend of navigational blunders, fuel weariness, and the difficult weather conditions probably added to the unit's vanishing. This episode features this present reality challenges that pilots and guides face while exploring through the Atlantic, particularly in areas inclined to unpredictable weather conditions.

Human mistake is another variable that figures noticeably in the logical assessment of episodes in the Bermuda Triangle. Navigational mix-ups, miscommunications, and mistakes in judgment can add to mishaps and vanishings. On account of Flight 19, Lieutenant Charles Taylor's navigational blunders and the inability to appropriately execute standard methodology for distinguishing their area assumed a vital part in the group's destiny.

The twentieth and 21st hundreds of years have seen huge progressions in innovation that have upgraded the security of oceanic and aeronautics route. Current vessels and airplane are outfitted with refined route frameworks, specialized gadgets, and wellbeing highlights that give more noteworthy strength against unanticipated difficulties. GPS innovation, specifically, has altered route, offering exact area data that is less helpless to attractive abnormalities.

In oceanic wellbeing, associations like the Global Sea Association (IMO) have laid out severe wellbeing principles and conventions to guarantee the prosperity of sailors and the security of sea transportation. Worked on weather conditions anticipating, satellite correspondence, and search and protect abilities further add to improved security adrift.

The vanishing of the SS El Faro in 2015 gives a contextual analysis in the job of human mistake and mechanical impediments. The freight transport experienced Typhoon Joaquin, a strong Classification 4 tempest, and eventually sank. The examination uncovered that the vessel had cruised into the way of the tropical storm because of a blend of elements, including obsolete climate data and the commander's independent direction.

While the occurrence was appalling, it highlighted the significance of informed navigation, particularly notwithstanding outrageous atmospheric conditions. The illustrations gained from such occurrences add to continuous endeavors to further develop wellbeing measures and upgrade the versatility of vessels working in testing conditions.

One normal confusion related with the Bermuda Triangle is the possibility that it is a district where unprecedented or strange peculiarities happen with more prominent recurrence than in different regions of the planet. In any case, while examining the authentic record of occurrences, it becomes apparent that the Bermuda Triangle doesn't encounter an abnormally large number of mishaps or vanishings contrasted with other vigorously voyaged oceanic and avionics courses.

Measurable investigations have exhibited that the pace of episodes inside the Bermuda Triangle is predictable with or even lower than that of other comparably bustling areas. The view of the Bermuda Triangle as an especially unsafe region is a result of particular detailing, sentimentality, and the enhancement of baffling stories. At the point when considered with regards to worldwide oceanic and aeronautics exercises, the Bermuda Triangle doesn't stand apart as a bizarrely perilous zone.

The absence of true acknowledgment of the Bermuda Triangle as a particular geographic area by global oceanic associations further difficulties the idea that it has one of a kind or extraordinary characteristics. The limits of the Bermuda Triangle are not all around settled upon, and various sources give various meanings of its area. The shortfall of a normalized assignment mirrors mainstream researchers' affirmation that the locale's standing is more established in fantasy and legends than in exact proof.

All in all, the logical assessment of the Bermuda Triangle uncovers that a significant number of the revealed episodes can be made sense of through a blend of normal peculiarities, human mistake, and natural elements. Attractive abnormalities, unfavorable atmospheric conditions, and mechanical limits add to the difficulties looked by guides in the district. Methane hydrate ejections, while experimentally conceivable, need adequate proof to help their job as a boundless reason for vanishings.

The utilization of measurable examinations further scatters the idea that the Bermuda Triangle is extraordinarily risky contrasted with other vigorously dealt regions. The locale's standing is, to a huge degree, a result of specific detailing, drama, and the propagation of fantasies and legends. As how we might interpret science and innovation progresses, the secrets of the Bermuda Triangle progressively respect judicious clarifications grounded in proof and reason.

While the Bermuda Triangle keeps on catching the public's creative mind, it is crucial for approach the subject with a basic outlook, perceiving the interaction between genuine difficulties and the persevering through charm of the unexplored world. Logical request and a pledge to confirm based clarifications give a pathway to demystifying the Bermuda Triangle and dispersing the misinterpretations that have encircled it for quite a long time. In doing as such, we explore the waters of legend and reality, isolating the unmistakable from the speculative and cultivating a more profound comprehension of the intricacies inborn in sea and flying investigation.

The Bermuda Triangle, a district in the western piece of the North Atlantic Sea, has for quite some time been inseparable from baffling events and unexplained peculiarities. Throughout the long term, a plenty of fantasies and legends have woven an enthralling story around this area, prompting broad hypothesis and misguided judgments. This investigation plans to dig into the events related with the Bermuda Triangle and, in doing as such, scatter normal confusions that have added to its persona.

One of the most well known events connected to the Bermuda Triangle is the vanishing of Flight 19 in December 1945. The unit, comprising of five U.S. Naval force planes on a standard preparation mission, evaporated suddenly. Driven by Lieutenant Charles Taylor, the planes became confused over the Atlantic, ran out of fuel, and were gone forever. This occurrence turned into a point of convergence in molding the Bermuda Triangle's cryptic standing.

Logically, the vanishing of Flight 19 can be credited to a mix of variables. Navigational blunders, unfavorable weather patterns, and fuel fatigue were recognized as likely explanations. The Bermuda Triangle's attractive irregularities, prompting disparities in compass readings, logical added to the group's confusion. While the destruction of Flight 19 has never been found, resulting examinations and examinations highlight the job of human and ecological variables in the occurrence.

A typical confusion encompassing the Bermuda Triangle is the possibility that it is a particular and obvious geographic region with one of a kind properties that make it more inclined to strange events. In all actuality, the expression "Bermuda Triangle" isn't formally acknowledged by worldwide oceanic associations, and its limits are not generally settled upon. The district's standing is to a great extent a result of legend and fables as opposed to a logically depicted space with particular qualities.

One more outstanding event related with the Bermuda Triangle is the vanishing of the USS Cyclops in Walk 1918. The USS Cyclops, a U.S. Naval force freight transport, evaporated with its 309 group individuals while in transit from Barbados to Baltimore. Different speculations have been proposed to make sense of its vanishing, including the chance of a German submarine assault or underlying disappointment. Regardless of broad pursuit endeavors, no destruction or trash from the USS Cyclops has at any point been found.

Deductively, the vanishing of the USS Cyclops stays a perplexing problem, and the absence of definitive proof has added to its persevering through puzzle. Nonetheless, crediting the occurrence to the Bermuda Triangle's alleged magical properties misrepresents the complicated idea of oceanic vanishings, which can result from a scope of variables, including navigational mistakes, outrageous climate, and mechanical disappointments.

One normal misguided judgment includes the idea that the Bermuda Triangle is a locale where compasses and other navigational instruments glitch because of puzzling powers. While the facts really confirm that the Bermuda Triangle encounters attractive irregularities, these inconsistencies are not novel to the area. Attractive declination, the point between evident north and attractive north, differs all around the world, and navigational diagrams are consistently refreshed to represent these varieties.

The presence of attractive oddities in the Bermuda Triangle can prompt navigational difficulties, particularly on the off chance that pilots or mariners neglect to likewise change their instruments. Nonetheless, crediting compass breakdowns exclusively to the Bermuda Triangle ignores the more extensive setting of worldwide attractive varieties. Moreover, current route frameworks, including GPS innovation, have to a great extent moderated the effect of attractive inconsistencies on oceanic and flying exercises.

In October 2015, the SS El Faro, a freight transport, turned into the focal point of consideration when it vanished nearby Tropical storm

Joaquin. The boat, with a team of 33, was in transit from Jacksonville, Florida, to San Juan, Puerto Rico. The examination concerning the SS El Faro's vanishing uncovered that the vessel had cruised straightforwardly into the way of the strong typhoon. The occurrence highlighted the effect of serious atmospheric conditions on oceanic wellbeing.

Deductively, the SS El Faro's vanishing is credited to a mix of variables, including the skipper's choice to explore through the typhoon, the age and underlying issues of the vessel, and the powerful idea of hurricanes. While the episode was heartbreaking, it was not characteristic of secretive or heavenly powers at play in the Bermuda Triangle. All things considered, it featured this present reality challenges presented by outrageous climate occasions in untamed ocean route.

The possibility that the Bermuda Triangle is a district where airplane and boats disappear suddenly, leaving no destruction or garbage, is an inescapable misguided judgment. Truly, examinations concerning sea and aeronautics occurrences inside the Bermuda Triangle have frequently uncovered legitimate and logically reasonable clarifications. Destruction and trash have been tracked down as a rule, testing the thought of unexplainable vanishings.

For example, the vanishing of Flight 19 was at first blurred in secret, yet ensuing examinations revealed proof of navigational mistakes and unfavorable weather patterns. Also, the destruction of the SS El Faro was found around three miles underneath the sea surface, giving basic insights about the conditions of its sinking. These episodes show the significance of exhaustive examinations in scattering confusions and unwinding the intricacies of sea and avionics vanishings.

The Bermuda Triangle has been connected to fantasies and legends including extraterrestrial movement and outsider kidnappings. A few stories propose that UFOs or unidentified flying items regular the locale, adding to vanishings and secretive peculiarities. While reports of UFO sightings exist, mainstream researchers underscores the requirement for solid proof to help cases of extraterrestrial inclusion.

The relationship between the Bermuda Triangle and extraterrestrial action depends on narrative records and unconfirmed observer declaration. The absence of exact proof and the commonness of normal and human-related clarifications for occurrences inside the Bermuda Triangle cast uncertainty on the legitimacy of extraterrestrial hypotheses. Logical request focuses on undeniable information, and until convincing proof is introduced, ascribing baffling events to outsiders stays speculative.

A pervasive logical point of view on the Bermuda Triangle includes the presence of enormous pits on the sea depths, frequently connected with methane hydrate ejections. Methane hydrates are ice-like designs containing methane gas that structure in unambiguous seabed silt. The hypothesis recommends that abrupt arrivals of methane gas can make shakiness in the water, prompting vicious emissions that upset the lightness of boats and influence them to quickly sink.

While the methane hydrate hypothesis gives a conceivable logical clarification to a few sea occurrences, it has constraints. Right off the bat, there is restricted exact proof to help the possibility that monstrous methane hydrate ejections happen regularly in the Bermuda Triangle.

Besides, the hypothesis fundamentally addresses sea vanishings and doesn't represent the episodes including airplane.

Moreover, research has uncovered that huge pits on the sea depths related with methane hydrate ejections are not restrictive to the Bermuda Triangle. Comparable developments have been found in different areas of the planet, testing the idea that the district has remarkable qualities as far as methane hydrate action. Mainstream researchers recognizes the likely job of methane hydrates at times however alerts against overgeneralizing their importance in making sense of the Bermuda Triangle's secrets.

The Mary Celeste, a vendor transport found loose and deserted in the Atlantic Sea in 1872, has been related with the Bermuda Triangle regardless of the episode happening outside the district. The boat was tracked down by the group of another vessel, the Dei Gratia, off the bank of the Azores. The Mary Celeste was generally flawless, with indications of a rushed takeoff, like to some degree spread out sails and a missing raft. Be that as it may, the freight and individual effects of the team were generally undisturbed.

The Mary Celeste is many times refered to act as an illustration of a vessel that evaporated suddenly, adding to the Bermuda Triangle's persona. Be that as it may, the occurrence happened in an alternate area, and ensuing examinations uncovered conceivable clarifications, including the chance of navigational blunders, robbery, or unfairness. The relationship of the Mary Celeste with the Bermuda Triangle shows how episodes outside the locale can become laced with its folklore.

All in all, the events related with the Bermuda Triangle, when inspected through a logical focal point, uncover a mind boggling exchange of normal powers, human variables, and natural circumstances. Unraveling the secrets from the legends is vital for grasping the district's world. Navigational mistakes, antagonistic atmospheric conditions, mechanical limits, and the unique idea of the untamed ocean add to the difficulties looked by sailors and pilots in the Bermuda Triangle.

Dissipating normal confusions includes tending to the specific announcing and sentimentality that have filled the Bermuda Triangle's persona. Logical clarifications, like attractive peculiarities, antagonistic climate, and human mistake, give sane experiences into the episodes credited to the locale. While certain secrets stay strange, the quest for information and a promise to prove based clarifications add to demystifying the Bermuda Triangle.

Chapter 5

"Shipwrecks and Sunken Treasures"

In the chronicles of oceanic history, the stories of wrecks and submerged treasures have long charmed the creative mind of globe-trotters, antiquarians, and visionaries the same. These accounts, frequently covered in secret and interest, unfurl across the huge region of the world's seas, each wreck addressing a novel section in the continuous adventure of human investigation and marine.

The appeal of submerged treasures lies not just in the material abundance that might lie underneath the sea's surface yet additionally in the tales of human victory and misfortune that go with these lowered relics of the past. From old vessels lost in the fogs of time to current sea calamities, the sea floor hides an abundance of mysteries ready to be found by bold pioneers and archeologists.

Perhaps of the most popular wreck in history is that of the RMS Titanic. In the early long periods of April 15, 1912, the "resilient" extravagance liner struck a chunk of ice and sank to the frigid profundities of the North Atlantic. The appalling loss of north of 1,500 lives stunned the world and made a permanent imprint on sea history. For a really long time, the Titanic stayed unseen, an eerie mystery at the lower part of the sea.

It was only after 1985 that the destruction of the Titanic was at long last situated by oceanographer Robert Ballard. The revelation, made conceivable by propels in remote ocean investigation innovation, uncovered the boat's broken remaining parts dispersed across the sea depths. The relics recuperated from the site gave an impactful look into the existences of the people who died on that game changing evening, as well as the extravagance of the actual boat.

The Titanic's story is only one illustration of the endless wrecks that speck the sea scene. A vessels met their death because of cataclysmic events like tempests and reefs, while others surrendered to human mistake, fighting, or theft. Each wreck tells a novel story, revealing insight into the conditions that prompted its death and the lives it influenced.

One such story hails from the Time of Investigation when European powers sent armadas across strange waters looking for new shipping lanes and domains. The slippery oceans asserted many boats during this time, their wooden structures surrendering to the whirlwinds that seethed across the untamed sea. The leftovers of these vessels lay secret underneath the waves, quiet observers to the trying undertakings of the individuals who cruised into the unexplored world.

In the waters off the shore of Florida, a submerged fortune of an alternate kind anticipates revelation — the remaining parts of Spanish vessels loaded down with gold and silver from the New World. These boats, known as the Spanish fortune armadas, were entrusted with shipping the abundance of the Americas back to Spain. Notwithstanding, their unsafe excursions frequently finished in calamity, as tempests and privateers hid along the course.

The waters of the Caribbean are especially wealthy in sea history, with endless wrecks lying underneath the sky blue surface. The stories of privateers and privateers who pillaged the oceans during the Brilliant Period of Robbery add a component of brave experience to the district's sea legend. The unbelievable privateer Blackbeard, whose genuine name was Edward Educate, met his end in these waters, and his lead, the Sovereign Anne's Vengeance, is among the submerged fortunes looked for by advanced voyagers.

As innovation propels, so too does our capacity to investigate the sea profundities and reveal the mysteries concealed inside its void. Submarines outfitted with cutting edge imaging and exhuming devices empower analysts to dive further than any time in recent memory, stripping back the layers of time that cover submerged ships and their valuable freight.

The mission for submerged treasures isn't simply a cutting edge pursuit; it has profound verifiable roots. In the nineteenth 100 years, the revelation of the disaster area of the Mary Rose off the shore of Britain gave a window into Tudor maritime history. The Mary Rose, a warship dispatched by Lord Henry VIII, sank in 1545 during a commitment with the French armada. The strikingly very much saved curios recuperated from the site offer a brief look into life on board a sixteenth century warship and the maritime fighting strategies of the time.

In the most distant ranges of the Pacific Sea, the destruction of the USS Indianapolis lies as a serious sign of the human expense of war. The weighty cruiser, which assumed a basic part in conveying parts of the nuclear bomb during The Second Great War, was destroyed by a Japanese submarine in 1945. The boat sank quickly, and many mariners were left abandoned in shark-pervaded waters for quite a long time before salvage endeavors were started. The disclosure of the Indianapolis wreck in 2017 carried conclusion to the groups of the people who died, as well as a restored interest in the boat's verifiable importance.

The draw of submerged treasures reaches out past the domain of authentic antiques to incorporate significant cargoes lost to the profundities. The sea floor is a storehouse of untold wealth, from valuable metals and gemstones to flavors and exchange products. The extremely old wrecks that speck the sea map are a demonstration of the financial and social trades that molded the course of mankind's set of experiences.

Off the bank of Namibia, the jewel fields of the Atlantic Sea hold the leftovers of precious stone mining tasks from the mid twentieth 100 years. Jewel rich stores were found on the sea floor, provoking an excited race to remove the valuable stones. The activity, notwithstanding, was laden with difficulties, and many mining vessels met their downfall in the fierce waters. Today, the indented stays of these precious stone dredgers act as a quiet demonstration of the charm and hazards of submerged asset extraction.

The quest for submerged treasures isn't without debate, as moral contemplations come to the front. The subject of proprietorship and the freedoms to rescue differ starting with one purview then onto the next. A few contend that submerged boats and their items ought to be protected as social legacy, while others see the potential for monetary increase through capable rescue tasks.

The narrative of the SS Focal America epitomizes the legitimate and moral intricacies encompassing submerged treasures. This side-wheel liner, weighed down with gold from the California Dash for unheard of wealth, sank off the bank of North Carolina in 1857. For more than 100 years, the boat and its freight stayed lost to the ocean. In the late twentieth hundred years, a privately owned business, Columbus-America Revelation Gathering, found the destruction and started rescue tasks.

The fights in court that followed brought up issues about the freedoms of salvors versus the privileges of the first proprietors and guarantors. Eventually, the salvors were granted a huge part of the recuperated treasure, reigniting banters about the legitimate harmony between confidential endeavor and the safeguarding of verifiable curios.

While the quest for submerged cherishes frequently centers around significant cargoes and valuable metals, the genuine lavishness lies in the accounts these wrecks tell about the human experience. Every vessel, whether a warship, dealer vessel, or pilgrim's leader, conveyed with it the expectations, dreams, and battles of the individuals who cruised on board. The relics recuperated from these disaster areas give an unmistakable connection to the past, offering a brief look into the regular routines, innovations, and societies of former periods.

In the Baltic Ocean, the very much protected wreck of the Vasa, a seventeenth century Swedish warship, remains as a demonstration of the crossing point of workmanship, designing, and misfortune. The Vasa, expected to be the pride of the Swedish armada, sank on its launch in 1628 because of configuration imperfections that made it cumbersome. Found during the 1950s and carefully raised from the profundities, the boat currently lives in the Vasa Gallery in Stockholm, where guests can wonder about its complicated carvings and find out about the conditions of its disastrous journey.

Progressions in marine prehistoric studies have extended how we might interpret old human advancements through the investigation of lowered urban communities and harbors. The depressed city of Thonis-Heracleion, off the bank of Egypt, was once a clamoring port in the Nile Delta during the hour of the pharaohs. Lowered for north of 1,000 years, the city's remains uncover an abundance of archeological fortunes, including sculptures, stoneware, and strict relics, giving significant bits of knowledge into the exchange of old Egyptian and Greek societies.

In the Aegean Ocean, the antiquated city of Pavlopetri lies lowered, its remains tracing all the way back to the Bronze Age. The surprisingly protected design of roads, structures, and yards offers an uncommon look into metropolitan preparation and day to day existence in a general public that originates before the Mycenaean progress. Marine archeologists utilize cutting edge innovations, for example, sonar planning and submerged unearthing to uncover the mysteries of Pavlopetri without upsetting the fragile submerged climate.

The secrets of submerged treasures reach out past the earthly domain to the investigation of room. The quest for extraterrestrial relics and remainders of old inestimable civic establishments is an idea that has caught the minds of researchers and sci-fi fans the same. While the possibility of submerged treasures in space might appear to be speculative, the mission for understanding our vast starting points and likely indications of keen extraterrestrial life keeps on driving investigation and exploration.

Back on The planet, the charm of submerged treasures has prompted the improvement of a subculture of fortune trackers and globe-trotters, each determined by the possibility of finding the following incredible oceanic secret. Submerged archeologists, outfitted with specific information and state of the art innovation, attempt dangerous excursions to investigate the sea profundities and open the privileged insights held inside submerged ships.

One such cutting edge traveler is Barry Clifford, whose endeavors have prompted the disclosure of a few generally huge wrecks. Clifford's most remarkable find is the Whydah Gally, a privateer transport that sank off the bank of Cape Cod in 1717. Loaded down with treasure looted from ships in the Atlantic, the Whydah turned into the leader of the famous privateer "Dark Sam" Bellamy. Clifford's disclosure of the Whydah wreck in 1984 uncovered a stash of curios, including gold coins, weapons, and individual things, giving an uncommon look into the brilliant period of robbery.

The charm of submerged treasures has likewise led to an expanding industry of marine rescue organizations having some expertise in the recuperation of significant cargoes from the sea floor. These organizations utilize trend setting innovations like remotely worked vehicles (ROVs) and independent submerged vehicles (AUVs) to study and unearth wrecks at profundities that were once unavailable. The business part of fortune hunting, in any case, carries with it a large group of moral contemplations and lawful difficulties.

The questionable instance of the SS Republic features the intricacies of business rescue activities. This Nationwide conflict time steamship sank off the bank of Georgia in 1865 while conveying a freight of coins and curios. Odyssey Marine Investigation, a confidential rescue organization, found the disaster area in 2003 and effectively recuperated a huge part of the boat's freight. Fights in court followed over the proprietorship freedoms, with the U.S. government and the first guarantors stating cases to the recuperated treasure.

The strain between the craving for authentic safeguarding and the quest for benefit highlights the continuous discussion encompassing the morals of submerged treasure recuperation. Advocates for capable rescue contend that the monetary motivators given by business rescue activities can finance further investigation and exploration, at last adding to how we might interpret history. Pundits, nonetheless, battle that the commercialization of submerged paleohistory represents a danger to the conservation of social legacy.

As of late, worldwide endeavors have been made to lay out rules and guidelines for the capable investigation and removal of submerged treasures. The UNESCO Show on the Security of the Submerged Social Legacy, embraced in 2001, looks to figure out some kind of harmony between the protection of submerged social legacy and the assistance of logical exploration and community. The show urges coordinated effort among countries to secure and oversee lowered archeological destinations.

In spite of the difficulties and discussions, the mission for submerged treasures keeps on driving development in marine innovation and investigation. The improvement of more modern submerged mechanical technology, high level imaging frameworks, and non-meddling uncovering strategies permits analysts to investigate wrecks with more prominent accuracy and insignificant effect on the general climate.

The submerged fortunes that lie underneath the sea's surface are windows into the past as well as storehouses of logical information. The investigation of marine prehistoric studies gives bits of knowledge into old shipbuilding strategies, shipping lanes, and route techniques. The investigation of antiquities recuperated from wrecks offers pieces of information about the way of life that created them, revealing insight into the interconnectedness of social orders across the oceans.

The submerged world remaining parts an immense wilderness of disclosure, with incalculable wrecks anticipating investigation. From the frigid profundities of the Cold to the sun-doused coral reefs of the Pacific, each lowered artifact recounts to a story that improves how we might interpret the human excursion across the seas. The safeguarding of these submerged fortunes requires a sensitive harmony between investigation, protection, and instruction.

As we leave on future endeavors to reveal the mysteries of the profound, moving toward the investigation of submerged treasures with a feeling of obligation and regard for the past is fundamental. The sea, with its secrets and fortunes, fills in as a period case that protects the traditions of the people who cruised its surface. In our journey to disentangle the tales of wrecks and submerged treasures, let us endeavor to be stewards of the ocean, guaranteeing that the marvels concealed underneath its waves persevere for a long time into the future.

5.1 Exploration of famous shipwrecks and lost treasures hidden in the deep sea.

The investigation of renowned wrecks and buried treasures concealed in the remote ocean has been a pursuit that traverses hundreds of years, powered by a strong mix of interest, verifiable interest, and the charm of wealth hid underneath the sea's surface. These oceanic secrets, dispersed across the globe, have enraptured the personalities of explorers, archeologists, and fortune trackers the same, each attempting to uncover the mysteries lowered in the watery profundities.

Perhaps of the most notable and heartbreaking wreck in history is that of the RMS Titanic. The epic sea liner, considered "resilient," met its awkward end in the bone chilling waters of the North Atlantic on April 15, 1912, in the wake of crashing into a chunk of ice. The sinking of the Titanic killed more than 1,500 travelers and team individuals and sent shockwaves through the world. For quite a long time, the area of the Titanic's resting place stayed a secret, an eerie riddle hiding underneath the sea's surface.

In 1985, oceanographer Robert Ballard, furnished with state of the art remote ocean investigation innovation, found the destruction of the Titanic, dispersed across the sea floor. The track down offered an impactful look into the result of the catastrophe, with the boat's broken remaining parts filling in as a quiet demonstration of the delicacy of human undertakings despite nature's power. The curios recuperated from the Titanic's watery grave gave an unmistakable association with the lives lost on that critical evening and the plushness of mid twentieth century transoceanic travel.

Past the awfulness of the Titanic, the world's seas hold a bunch of wrecks, each with its own story of win or misfortune. The Time of Investigation, a period traversing the fifteenth to the seventeenth hundreds of years, saw European powers sending armadas across unknown waters looking for new shipping lanes and domains. The risky oceans asserted many boats during this period, their wooden bodies capitulating to tempests, reefs, and the vulnerabilities of the vast sea.

Off the shore of Florida, the leftovers of Spanish ships offer a brief look into the sea misfortunes of the past. The Spanish fortune armadas, entrusted with shipping the wealth of the Americas to Spain, frequently confronted tempests, robbery, and the misleading waters of the Caribbean. The submerged fortunes that lie underneath the purplish blue surface of these waters recount an account of extravagant cargoes lost to the profundities, ready to be rediscovered by present day pioneers.

In the Caribbean, the stories of privateers and privateers add a brave aspect to the district's oceanic history. The famous privateer Blackbeard, whose genuine name was Edward Educate, met his end in these waters, and his leader, the Sovereign Anne's Retribution, is among the submerged fortunes looked for by contemporary globe-trotters. The legends of covered privateer gold and secret fortunes keep on powering the creative mind, for certain trying spirits setting out on journeys to unwind the secrets of the great oceans.

Progressions in innovation play had a vital impact in the investigation of these submerged time containers. Subs furnished with cutting edge imaging and unearthing instruments permit analysts to dig further than any time in recent memory, stripping back the layers of time that cover submerged ships and their valuable freight. The mission for submerged treasures isn't just a cutting edge pursuit; it has profound verifiable roots.

The nineteenth century saw the disclosure of the disaster area of the Mary Rose off the shore of Britain, giving a window into Tudor maritime history. The Mary Rose, a warship charged by Lord Henry VIII, sank in 1545 during a commitment with the French armada. The surprisingly very much saved curios recuperated from the site offer experiences into life on board a sixteenth century warship and the maritime fighting strategies of the time.

In the Pacific Sea, the destruction of the USS Indianapolis fills in as a grave sign of the human expense of battle during The Second Great War. The weighty cruiser, which assumed a basic part in conveying parts of the nuclear bomb, was obliterated by a Japanese submarine in 1945. The boat sank quickly, leaving many mariners abandoned in shark-pervaded waters for quite a long time. The disclosure of the Indianapolis wreck in 2017 carried conclusion to the groups of the people who died and restored interest in the boat's verifiable importance.

The investigation of submerged treasures stretches out past the domain of authentic ancient rarities to incorporate important cargoes lost to the profundities. Off the shore of Namibia, the jewel fields of the Atlantic Sea hold the remainders of precious stone mining tasks from the mid twentieth 100 years. The disclosure of jewel rich stores on the sea floor started a hurry to extricate the valuable stones, prompting the sinking of many mining vessels in the fierce waters. Today, the depressed remaining parts of these jewel dredgers act as quiet observers to the difficulties and appeal of submerged asset extraction.

Nonetheless, the quest for submerged treasures isn't without discussion. Moral contemplations come to the very front, with inquiries of possession and the privileges to rescue differing starting with one locale then onto the next. The narrative of the SS Focal America epitomizes the lawful and moral intricacies encompassing submerged treasure recuperation.

This steamship, loaded down with gold from the California Dash for unheard of wealth, sank off the shore of North Carolina in 1857. For north of 100 years, the boat and its freight stayed lost to the ocean. In the late twentieth hundred years, a privately owned business, Columbus-America Disclosure Gathering, found the destruction and started rescue tasks. Fights in court resulted, bringing up issues about the privileges of salvors versus the freedoms of the first proprietors and safety net providers. The salvors were eventually granted a huge piece of the recuperated treasure, igniting banters about the harmony between confidential endeavor and the protection of verifiable curios.

The intricacies of business rescue activities are additionally exemplified by the dubious instance of the SS Republic. This Nationwide conflict time steamship sank off the shore of Georgia in 1865 while conveying a freight of coins and curios.

Odyssey Marine Investigation, a confidential rescue organization, found the disaster area in 2003 and effectively recuperated a significant part of the boat's freight. Fights in court resulted over proprietorship freedoms, with the U.S. government and the first back up plans declaring cases to the recuperated treasure. The strain between the longing for verifiable conservation and the quest for benefit highlights the continuous discussion encompassing the morals of submerged treasure recuperation.

Worldwide endeavors have been made to lay out rules and guidelines for the dependable investigation and uncovering of submerged treasures. The UNESCO Show on the Assurance of the Submerged Social Legacy, embraced in 2001, tries to adjust the conservation of submerged social legacy with logical examination and community. The show urges coordinated effort among countries to safeguard and oversee lowered archeological locales.

Regardless of the difficulties and debates, the journey for submerged treasures keeps on driving advancement in marine innovation and investigation. The improvement of more refined submerged mechanical technology, high level imaging frameworks, and non-nosy exhuming strategies permits scientists to investigate wrecks with more noteworthy accuracy and insignificant effect on the general climate.

The submerged world remaining parts a huge outskirts of revelation, with innumerable wrecks anticipating investigation. From the cold profundities of the Icy to the sun-doused coral reefs of the Pacific, each lowered artifact recounts to a story that improves how we might interpret the human excursion across the seas. The protection of these submerged fortunes requires a fragile harmony between investigation, preservation, and schooling.

As we set out on future undertakings to reveal the mysteries of the profound, moving toward the investigation of submerged treasures with a feeling of obligation and regard for the past is fundamental. The sea, with its secrets and fortunes, fills in as a period container that protects the traditions of the people who cruised its surface. In our mission to unwind the tales of wrecks and buried treasures concealed in the remote ocean, let us endeavor to be stewards of the ocean, guaranteeing that the marvels concealed underneath its waves persevere for a long time into the future.

5.2 Accounts of successful underwater archaeology and salvage operations.

The field of submerged paleontology and rescue tasks has seen various victories in uncovering the secrets of lowered history. These undertakings, set apart by inventiveness, innovative advances, and a profound appreciation for saving the past, have exposed fortunes, relics, and experiences that were once concealed underneath the sea's surface.

One prominent example of overcoming adversity in submerged antiquarianism is the revelation and unearthing of the antiquated city of Pavlopetri off the shore of Laconia in Greece. Pavlopetri, tracing all the way back to the Bronze Age, is viewed as quite possibly of the most established lowered city on the planet. Found in 1967 by Dr. Nicholas Flemming, the city's exact design, complete with roads, structures, and yards, challenges traditional thoughts about metropolitan preparation during that time.

Soon after its revelation, submerged archeologists, including Dr. Jon Henderson, have used cutting edge innovations, for example, sonar planning and remotely worked vehicles (ROVs) to investigate and report Pavlopetri. The discoveries give an extraordinary window into the day to day routine and design of a general public that originates before the Mycenaean progress. Pavlopetri remains as a demonstration of the extraordinary capacities of submerged paleontology in disentangling the mysteries of old civic establishments.

One more milestone accomplishment in submerged paleontology is the removal of the Antikythera Wreck. Found by wipe jumpers off the shoreline of the Greek island of Antikythera in 1901, the wreck yielded a remarkable gathering of old relics, including sculptures, coins, and a mysterious mechanical gadget known as the Antikythera Component. The Component, an old simple PC, is viewed as one of the main archeological revelations of the twentieth 100 years.

More than hundred years after its underlying disclosure, a group of jumpers and archeologists, drove by Brendan Foley, set out on an exhaustive re-investigation of the Antikythera Wreck in the mid 21st 100 years. Utilizing progressed jumping innovation and ROVs, the group uncovered extra fortunes and relics, revealing new insight into the boat's freight and the social trade that occurred in the Mediterranean during artifact. The continuous investigation of the Antikythera Wreck embodies how current innovation can improve the comprehension of old oceanic history.

In the domain of warship paleohistory, the recuperation of the Swedish warship Vasa remains as a demonstration of fastidious exhuming and conservation endeavors. The Vasa, which sank on its first venture in 1628, was rescued from the profundities of Stockholm's harbor in the twentieth 100 years. The disaster area's safeguarding and possible presentation in the Vasa Exhibition hall feature the cooperative endeavors of marine archeologists, designers, and conservators.

The revelation of the Confederate submarine H.L. Hunley off the bank of South Carolina denoted a huge leap forward in the field of oceanic paleontology. Lost in 1864 during the American Nationwide conflict subsequent to turning into the main submarine to sink a foe warship, the Hunley remained covered in secret for more than 100 years. In 2000, under the heading of excavator Dr. Mark M. Newell, the submarine was effectively raised from the sea depths.

The careful removal and preservation endeavors uncovered strikingly safeguarded subtleties of the Hunley, giving experiences into its plan, innovation, and the conditions of its sinking. The recuperation of the Hunley addresses an achievement in the use of cutting edge archeological strategies to uncover the mysteries of noteworthy maritime vessels.

An imperative progress in the domain of fortune recuperation comes from the uncovering of the Nuestra Señora de Atocha, a Spanish vessel that sank off the shore of Florida in 1622. Found by treasure tracker Mel Fisher in 1985, the Atocha's freight included gold, silver, emeralds, and other valuable antiquities. The fruitful rescue activity, known as the "Atocha Motherlode," positions among the main submerged treasure disclosures ever.

The Atocha's recuperation included long periods of careful unearthing and the execution of state of the art innovation, including side-filter sonar and metal finders. The revelation not just enhanced how we might interpret Spanish provincial exchange yet additionally ignited legitimate discussions over possession freedoms, with the territory of Florida, financial backers, and Fisher's organization participated in extended fights in court. The Atocha adventure highlights the intricacies and legitimate difficulties related with submerged treasure recuperation.

In the space of present day sea paleontology, the investigation of the German ship Bismarck addresses a wonderful accomplishment. Sunk during The Second Great War in 1941, the Bismarck's destruction lay unseen on the sea floor for almost 50 years. In 1989, oceanographer and marine prehistorian Dr. Robert Ballard, utilizing progressed remotely worked vehicles, found the Bismarck wreck more than 4,700 meters underneath the outer layer of the Atlantic Sea.

The resulting investigation and documentation of the Bismarck displayed the use of remote ocean innovation in uncovering the destiny of an unbelievable warship. The disaster area's condition gave bits of knowledge into the fight harm caused during its last commitment with the English Imperial Naval force. The Bismarck's revelation and assessment add to how we might interpret maritime fighting and the authentic occasions of The Second Great War.

The progress of these submerged paleohistory and rescue activities highlights the interdisciplinary idea of the field. Cooperation between archeologists, sea life researchers, history specialists, architects, and preservationists is significant for the outcome of such undertakings. The incorporation of state of the art innovation, from remotely worked vehicles to cutting edge imaging frameworks, has altered the capacity to investigate and report lowered destinations with uncommon accuracy.

In any case, the victories in submerged prehistoric studies likewise accompany moral contemplations and difficulties. The issue of possession and the freedoms to rescue frequently prompts fights in court and discussions over the commercialization of authentic antiquities.

Adjusting the quest for information with the safeguarding of social legacy stays a fragile and continuous undertaking.

As the field keeps on advancing, new outskirts in submerged prehistoric studies arise. The journey to uncover lowered urban areas, investigate old shipping lanes, and uncover the insider facts of lost developments drives specialists and pilgrims into unknown waters. Progresses in innovation, including computerized reasoning, 3D planning, and submerged drones, vow to additional upgrade our capacity to unwind the secrets concealed underneath the sea's surface.

The narratives of effective submerged paleohistory and rescue tasks rouse a feeling of miracle and interest in the huge and neglected domains underneath the waves. The conservation of our oceanic legacy, whether as antiquated wrecks, warships, or submerged treasures, depends on the devotion of the individuals who endeavor to comprehend the past while regarding the fragile biological systems of the submerged world.

As we keep on digging into the secrets of the profound, the stories of fruitful submerged archeological undertakings act as reference points directing us toward a more extravagant comprehension of our common mankind's set of experiences.

5.3 Discussion on the ethical considerations and challenges of preserving maritime heritage.

The safeguarding of sea legacy is an intricate undertaking loaded with moral contemplations and difficulties that length the domains of prehistoric studies, protection, trade, and lawful systems. As submerged archeologists and rescue administrators try to reveal the insider facts concealed underneath the sea's surface, they wrestle with the obligation of saving social legacy while exploring the dim waters of possession privileges, business interests, and natural effect.

One of the essential moral contemplations in sea legacy conservation spins around the topic of possession. At the point when a wreck or lowered site is found, figuring out who has the privilege to rescue or exhume turns into a sensitive and frequently combative issue. The lawful systems overseeing these issues can change generally among countries and are affected by peaceful accords and shows.

The UNESCO Show on the Security of the Submerged Social Legacy, embraced in 2001, looks to lay out a shared conviction for the security of lowered archeological locales. The show urges countries to coordinate in defending submerged social legacy, underscoring the significance of saving locales in situ whenever the situation allows. In any case, the test emerges when the interests of business salvors, archeologists, and states meet, prompting disagreements regarding possession and control.

The instance of the SS Focal America, a nineteenth century steamship conveying gold from the California Dash for unheard of wealth, epitomizes the moral intricacies encompassing proprietorship privileges.

Found in the late twentieth hundred years by a confidential rescue organization, Columbus-America Revelation Gathering, the disaster area turned into the subject of fights in court. The salvors were in the end granted a huge piece of the recuperated treasure, bringing up issues about the harmony between confidential venture and the protection of verifiable relics.

Business rescue activities, while frequently adding to the revelation and recuperation of significant antiques, additionally present moral situations. The quest for benefit can prompt sped up unearthing strategies, possibly making hopeless harm fragile archeological locales. The fortune driven rationale behind some rescue tasks has provoked worries about the prioritization of monetary profit over the protection of social legacy.

The instance of the SS Republic, a Nationwide conflict time steamship, features the strain between business interests and moral contemplations. Odyssey Marine Investigation, a confidential rescue organization, found the disaster area in 2003 and effectively recuperated a significant part of the boat's freight. Fights in court followed over proprietorship privileges, highlighting the requirement for a fragile harmony between the financial motivators of fortune recuperation and the moral basic of safeguarding verifiable curios.

Natural effect is one more basic moral thought in oceanic legacy safeguarding. Unearthing and rescue tasks can upset the fragile biological systems that have conformed to wrecks and lowered locales over many years or hundreds of years. The unsettling influence of residue, the arrival of poisons, and the actual effect of exhuming can lastingly affect marine life and submerged territories.

The significance of saving the submerged climate is exemplified by the situation of the RMS Titanic. While the disclosure of the Titanic wreck in 1985 was a fantastic accomplishment in submerged paleohistory, resulting undertakings and rescue endeavors thely affect the site. The utilization of submarines, remotely worked vehicles (ROVs), and monitored plunges to the Titanic has prompted the aggravation of the general climate and the expected loss of fragile antiques.

The moral contemplations encompassing natural effect stretch out past notable wrecks to include continuous investigations of submerged locales and lowered urban communities. The investigation of Pavlopetri, an old Bronze Age city off the shoreline of Greece, brings up issues about the possible impacts of removal on the submerged biological system. Scientists should cautiously adjust the quest for information with the need to limit disturbance to marine life and environments.

Notwithstanding the actual effect on the climate, the moral elements of oceanic legacy protection incorporate the obligation to regard and draw in with neighborhood networks.

The social meaning of submerged destinations frequently stretches out to the networks living in vicinity to these areas. Informed assent and cooperation with nearby partners are fundamental parts of moral safeguarding endeavors.

The investigation of the Antikythera Wreck off the bank of Greece fills in to act as an illustration of moral commitment with neighborhood networks. The continuous unearthings, drove by a worldwide group of archeologists, include joint effort with Greek specialists and nearby jumpers. This approach not just encourages a feeling of shared responsibility for social legacy yet in addition guarantees that the advantages of investigation reach out to the networks in question.

Adjusting the interests of different partners, including archeologists, salvors, states, and neighborhood networks, requires straightforward correspondence and moral direction. The field of sea legacy conservation is advancing, and moral rules are fundamental to explore the intricacies innate in the investigation of lowered destinations.

One part of sea legacy safeguarding that rises above individual wrecks or antiquities is the more extensive inquiry of how to address the combined effect of human exercises on submerged social legacy. As innovation progresses and submerged investigation turns out to be more available, the potential for disclosure and exhuming increments. Moral contemplations should stretch out past individual ventures to incorporate the combined impacts of far reaching investigation on the submerged archeological record.

The dependable utilization of innovation is a significant part of moral sea legacy conservation. High level imaging frameworks, including sonar planning and photogrammetry, permit analysts to archive and concentrate on lowered destinations without actually upsetting them. Non-meddling techniques, when relevant, ought to be focused on to limit the effect on the submerged climate and safeguard locales for people in the future.

Instruction and public effort are essential to the moral conservation of oceanic legacy. Expanding mindfulness about the significance of submerged social legacy, the difficulties it faces, and the moral contemplations engaged with its investigation can earn support from the general population, policymakers, and the scholarly local area. Public commitment likewise cultivates a feeling of shared liability regarding saving our sea legacy.

The moral contemplations encompassing sea legacy conservation are dynamic and require continuous discourse and joint effort. Worldwide participation, directed by moral systems, for example, the UNESCO show, assumes a urgent part in tending to the worldwide idea of submerged social legacy. The foundation of clear rules for the dependable investigation, removal, and conservation of lowered locales is vital to guaranteeing that the marvels concealed underneath the sea's surface persevere for people in the future.

As we explore the difficulties of safeguarding oceanic legacy, the moral goals of informed assent, ecological stewardship, and social responsiveness ought to direct our activities. Whether investigating old wrecks, revealing lost developments, or rescuing submerged treasures, a promise to moral practices guarantees that the quest for information happens as one with the protection of our common mankind's set of experiences. In the watery profundities where history lies lowered, the moral contemplations of oceanic legacy safeguarding become the compass directing our investigation and protection endeavors

The protection of sea legacy is a diverse test that envelops an expansive scope of issues, from ecological worries to legitimate intricacies and moral contemplations. As humankind endeavors to investigate, comprehend, and safeguard the remainders of its sea past, a few key difficulties arise, requesting cautious route and smart arrangements.

One of the essential difficulties in safeguarding sea legacy lies in the natural effect of investigation and rescue activities. Lowered destinations, including wrecks and antiquated harbors, frequently act as fake reefs, encouraging remarkable biological systems. Exhuming, digging, and other meddling exercises can upset these fragile conditions, prompting the possible loss of marine life and natural surroundings.

The instance of the RMS Titanic, apparently the most well known wreck ever, delineates the natural difficulties related with submerged investigation. While the disclosure of the Titanic wreck in 1985 denoted an achievement in sea prehistoric studies, resulting visits to the site have raised worries about the unsettling influence of the encompassing environment. The actual effect of subs, remotely worked vehicles (ROVs), and monitored jumps can have enduring outcomes on the submerged climate.

Past notorious wrecks, progressing investigation of lowered urban communities and antiquated ports presents comparable difficulties. The submerged city of Pavlopetri off the shoreline of Greece, tracing all the way back to the Bronze Age, is a demonstration of the likely wealth of lowered archeological destinations. In any case, the exhuming of such destinations requires cautious thought of the effect on marine life and environments. Scientists and progressives should explore the strain between the journey for information and the need to safeguard submerged conditions.

A connected test includes the possible loss of archeological setting because of clumsy rescue tasks. Wrecks are time containers that offer experiences into verifiable occasions, innovative progressions, and social practices. Notwithstanding, rushed or misguided unearthings can upset the layers of residue that have aggregated over hundreds of years, eradicating important context oriented data.

The Antikythera Wreck, found off the shore of Greece in 1901, is an illustration of a site that yielded an abundance of data because of cautious removal. The wreck, tracing all the way back to the first century BCE, contained the Antikythera Component, an old simple PC. Continuous unearthings, utilizing cutting edge innovations, for example, ROVs, intend to remove further bits of knowledge while safeguarding the trustworthiness of the site and its archeological setting.

Lawful difficulties further entangle the conservation of sea legacy. The proprietorship privileges to wrecks and their cargoes can be dependent upon complex lawful systems that differ among countries and districts. The UNESCO Show on the Assurance of the Submerged Social Legacy, embraced in 2001, tries to lay out rules for the security of lowered archeological destinations. Notwithstanding, the execution of these rules depends on the collaboration of individual countries, and disagreements regarding possession freedoms continue.

The instance of the SS Focal America, a nineteenth century steamship conveying gold from the California Dash for unheard of wealth, highlights the legitimate intricacies encompassing submerged social legacy. Found in the late twentieth hundred years by a confidential rescue organization, the disaster area turned into the subject of fights in court over proprietorship privileges to the recuperated treasure. The crossing point of business interests, public sway, and the protection of verifiable relics brings up issues about the job of lawful systems in adjusting contending concerns.

Business rescue tasks, driven by the commitment of finding significant antiques and fortunes, present one more layer of difficulties. While these tasks can add to the recuperation of verifiable things, they frequently work inside a benefit situated system that might focus on monetary profit over the safeguarding of social legacy. Assisted unearthing techniques, deficient preservation rehearses, and the commodification of curios can think twice about trustworthiness of submerged destinations.

The instance of the SS Republic, a Nationwide conflict time steamship, represents the moral and legitimate difficulties related with business rescue. Odyssey Marine Investigation, a confidential rescue organization, found the disaster area in 2003 and effectively recuperated a significant part of the boat's freight. Fights in court resulted over possession privileges, accentuating the requirement for moral contemplations in the commercialization of submerged paleohistory.

Moral contemplations assume a focal part in the conservation of oceanic legacy. Whether or not to leave a site in that frame of mind to recuperate relics for study and show includes a sensitive harmony between the quest for information and the preservation of verifiable assets. The UNESCO show urges countries to focus on in situ protection, perceiving the benefit of leaving lowered destinations immaculate whenever the situation allows.

The difficulties of moral direction are apparent in the continuous investigation of the antiquated city of Pavlopetri. The very much protected format of roads, structures, and yards presents a novel chance to concentrate on metropolitan preparation and day to day existence in a Bronze Age society. Be that as it may, the moral difficulty emerges in deciding the degree to which the site ought to be uncovered and whether certain regions ought to be left immaculate for people in the future with further developed advances.

Public effort and schooling comprise extra moral difficulties in sea legacy protection. Drawing in with nearby networks, bringing issues to light about the meaning of submerged social legacy, and cultivating a feeling of shared liability are significant parts of moral safeguarding endeavors. Joint effort with partners, including legislatures, specialists, and general society, guarantees that safeguarding drives think about different viewpoints and address the requirements of those straightforwardly impacted by oceanic legacy investigation.

The capable utilization of innovation is a vital part of moral conservation. High level imaging frameworks, for example, sonar planning and photogrammetry, empower scientists to archive lowered destinations without genuinely upsetting them. Non-meddling strategies, when relevant, ought to be focused on to limit the effect on the submerged climate and safeguard locales for people in the future.

The overall test in safeguarding sea legacy is to figure out some kind of harmony among investigation and preservation. As mechanical progressions keep on growing our ability to investigate the sea's profundities, the requirement for moral rules turns out to be progressively squeezing. The fragile dance between uncovering the privileged insights of the past and shielding the trustworthiness of submerged locales requires a smart and cooperative methodology.

As we defy the difficulties of safeguarding oceanic legacy, a general topic arises: the interconnectedness of natural, legitimate, and moral contemplations. The protection of submerged social legacy isn't exclusively a question of mechanical ability or legitimate systems; it is a nuanced and interdisciplinary undertaking that requests a comprehensive comprehension of the multifaceted trap of difficulties at play.

In exploring these difficulties, the field of sea legacy conservation is developing. Continuous discoursed among archeologists, moderates, lawful specialists, and nearby networks are vital for shape moral rules and best practices. The basic to safeguard the fortunes concealed underneath the sea's surface is a common obligation that rises above lines and teaches, requiring an aggregate obligation to stewardship and reasonable investigation.

Notwithstanding natural dangers, legitimate intricacies, and moral predicaments, the conservation of sea legacy remains as a demonstration of our commitment to understanding and protecting the rich embroidery of mankind's set of experiences.

The difficulties experienced along this excursion just highlight the significance of moving toward oceanic legacy conservation with lowliness, regard, and a significant acknowledgment of the interconnectedness between past, present, and future.

Chapter 6

"Underwater Mysteries and UFOs"

Far below the outer layer of our planet lies a tremendous and puzzling domain that has caught the creative mind of researchers, wayfarers, and intrigue scholars the same - the submerged world. As we dive into the profundities of the seas, we experience a huge number of marvels, from unusual and tricky animals to old wrecks and submerged urban communities. However, in the midst of the excellence and intricacy of the submerged domain, there are additionally secrets that oppose clarification, and none more charming than the diligent reports of unidentified flying items (UFOs) underneath the waves.

The seas cover over 70% of the World's surface, and a lot of their profundities stay neglected and obscure. The boundlessness and unavailability of the submerged world make it an ideal favorable place for hypothesis and creative mind. For a really long time, mariners have shared stories of ocean beasts and legendary animals sneaking in the profound, adding to the quality of secret that encompasses the seas. In any case, lately, as innovation has progressed and investigation has become more refined, the center has moved from legend to the real world, uncovering a large group of submerged secrets that challenge how we might interpret the world underneath the waves.

Quite possibly of the most perplexing peculiarity detailed in the profundities of the seas is the presence of unidentified lowered objects (USOs) - the amphibian partners to UFOs. While UFO sightings in the skies have been a subject of discussion and interest for a really long time, the possibility of baffling items moving underneath the sea's surface adds another layer of interest to the extraterrestrial speculation. Witnesses, including maritime faculty, submariners, and non military personnel jumpers, have depicted experiences with bizarre, quick items submerged that challenge the known capacities of human-made innovation.

The USO peculiarity is definitely not a new turn of events. Verifiable records going back hundreds of years recount mariners noticing uncommon lights, items, and even "flying boats" underneath the waves. In the cutting edge period, with the approach of submarines and high level submerged investigation gear, reports of USOs have become more itemized and various. A few observers portray seeing plate molded objects moving at inconceivable velocities, while others relate experiences with enormous submerged designs of obscure beginning.

The military, with its submarines and sonar innovation, has been at the very front of USO experiences. Declassified reports uncover cases where maritime vessels have recognized and followed submerged objects showing flighty way of behaving. These items frequently appear to outsmart even the most developed submarines, leaving specialists confounded about their conceivable beginning and reason.

One of the most notable episodes including USOs happened in 1971, when the USS Trepang, a US Naval force submarine, experienced an enormous submerged object nearby Iceland. As indicated by reports, the item was round and produced an odd greenish light. The submarine's group, including experienced submariners and officials, noticed the article for a few minutes before it quickly climbed to the surface and shot up high. The episode stays unexplained, and the authority reaction from the military was unclear, leaving space for hypothesis and paranoid fears.

Notwithstanding military experiences, regular people have likewise revealed USO sightings during remote ocean jumps and submarine investigation. In 1997, a group of scientists investigating the profundities of the Puerto Rico Channel, one of the most profound pieces of the Atlantic Sea, caught film of a unidentified item moving at extraordinary velocities. The item seemed to oppose the laws of physical science, provoking hypothesis about its starting point. Some proposed it very well may be a formerly obscure marine organic entity, while others engaged the possibility that it was a complex submerged vehicle of extraterrestrial beginning.

The investigation of the sea floor has additionally uncovered bewildering submerged structures that challenge how we might interpret history and antiquated civic establishments. Off the shoreline of Japan, for instance, analysts have found gigantic stone designs looking like pyramids.

These designs, situated at profundities that would have been unimaginable for people to work during old times, bring up issues about the chance of cutting edge civic establishments originating before our known history. The secret extends as analysts battle to make sense of how these designs became and what reason they could have served.

Also, off the shoreline of Cuba, sonar pictures stand out of scientists and intrigue scholars the same. These pictures uncover what gives off an impression of being an immense submerged city, complete with mathematically adjusted structures and pyramidal developments. The profundity of the designs recommends an age that originates before the known history of human development, driving some to estimate that they could be the remainders of a lost civilization or even proof of extraterrestrial contribution in Earth's far off past.

While standard science frequently approaches such cases with suspicion, the sheer volume of revealed sightings and the consistency of specific subtleties across various records make the submerged secrets challenging to altogether excuse. Researchers and scientists keep on wrestling with the restrictions of investigation innovation and our comprehension of the seas, perceiving that there is a lot of we presently can't seem to find underneath the waves.

As of late, progressions in submerged drone innovation and remotely worked vehicles (ROVs) have permitted analysts to investigate beforehand difficult to reach profundities with more noteworthy accuracy. These instruments have given staggering pictures and recordings of remote ocean environments and the odd animals that occupy them. However, even with these innovative headways, the submerged world remaining parts to a great extent strange, and the secrets continue.

The convergence of submerged secrets and UFO experiences brings up fascinating issues about the idea of these peculiarities and their possible associations. A few scholars suggest that specific USO sightings could be proof of submerged bases or stations worked by extraterrestrial creatures. The tremendousness of the seas, with their secret profundities and neglected domains, gives a helpful cover to any high level civilization or insight trying to stay undetected by mankind.

The possibility of extraterrestrial creatures working underneath the sea waves takes advantage of a profound well of human interest with the obscure and the powerful. It reverberations topics tracked down in sci-fi writing and movies, where outsider developments sneak in the most obscure corners of the Earth, stowed away from natural eyes. While such thoughts might appear to be unrealistic to standard science, the sheer number of revealed sightings and experiences requests a nearer assessment of the potential outcomes.

Notwithstanding USOs, there are reports of unidentified flying items progressing flawlessly between the skies and the seas. These occurrences, frequently depicted as "transmedium" UFOs, challenge our conventional comprehension of physical science and optimal design.

Witnesses have announced seeing UFOs that plunge into the sea and proceed with their flight submerged with next to no clear interruption to their development. This capacity to cross both air and water opposes the constraints of human-made airplane and proposes a degree of innovation past our momentum understanding.

One striking episode of a transmedium UFO happened in 2004 during the renowned Spasm Tac UFO experience. The experience included U.S. Naval force pilots from the USS Nimitz who noticed and drew in with unidentified flying items off the shoreline of California. The items, depicted as "Spasm Tac" formed, showed unprecedented flight capacities, remembering quick speed increase and unexpected shifts for course. In one occasion, a UFO was accounted for to have slid from the sky and entered the sea, vanishing suddenly.

The Spasm Tac UFO occurrence gathered huge consideration when the U.S. Division of Protection declassified and delivered video film caught by the Naval force pilots. The recording, alongside observer accounts, powered hypothesis about the nature and beginning of the items. A few specialists recommended progressed drone innovation or mystery military airplane as potential clarifications, while others engaged the chance of extraterrestrial inclusion.

The association among UFOs and submerged secrets reaches out past sightings and experiences. A few specialists recommend that there might be a relationship between's the areas of UFO sightings and submerged land highlights. The thought is that sure regions, for example, submerged channels, volcanic vents, or old designs, may act as focal points for extraterrestrial creatures or high level developments.

The Bermuda Triangle, a locale in the western piece of the North Atlantic Sea, is one such region that has for some time been related with baffling vanishings of boats and airplane. While the Bermuda Triangle's standing as a risk zone has been generally exposed, a few scholars recommend that the district's set of experiences of irregular occasions could be connected to the presence of submerged designs or peculiarities that draw in UFO movement.

Intriguingly, the Bermuda Triangle has likewise been the site of announced USO sightings. Witnesses guarantee to have seen unidentified articles entering and leaving the water at high paces, adding one more layer to the locale's persona. While logical clarifications, for example, regular methane hydrate ejections, have been proposed for a portion of the peculiarities related with the Bermuda Triangle, the intermingling of UFO sightings and submerged secrets stays a subject of hypothesis and discussion.

The quest for replies to the puzzler of submerged secrets and UFOs has prompted the arrangement of examination associations committed to researching these peculiarities. One such association is the Logical Alliance for UAP (Unidentified Ethereal Peculiarities) Studies, which means to carry a thorough logical way to deal with the investigation of UFOs.

The consideration of submerged viewpoints in UAP studies mirrors the acknowledgment that some UFO occurrences include associations with the seas.

As specialists and researchers dive into the information and onlooker accounts, they face the test of isolating authentic unexplained peculiarities from misidentifications, tricks, and mental elements. The shame encompassing UFO research, frequently excused as pseudoscience or fear inspired notion, adds an extra layer of intricacy to the examination. Regardless of these difficulties, there is a developing affirmation inside established researchers that specific UFO episodes request serious request.

Lately, states and military associations have made moves to destigmatize the investigation of UFOs and make recently characterized data available to general society. The U.S. government's affirmation of the presence of the High level Aviation Danger Distinguishing proof Program (AATIP) and the arrival of declassified UFO film address a huge change in straightforwardness. While these disclosures don't give conclusive responses, they open the entryway for additional examination and discourse on the idea of unidentified airborne peculiarities.

The convergence of submerged secrets and UFOs likewise raises moral and ecological contemplations. The seas, previously confronting various dangers from contamination, overfishing, and environmental change, presently stand up to the expected effect of cutting edge extraterrestrial or obscure advancements. The possibility of submerged bases or designs brings up issues about what such establishments could mean for marine life and environments. Analysts and policymakers should think about the ramifications of possible contact with non-human insights and the requirement for capable investigation and preservation of the seas.

The investigation of submerged secrets and UFOs stretches out past the domain of science and into mainstream society. Books, narratives, and movies have investigated the crossing point of these peculiarities, mixing logical request with inventive hypothesis. The charm of the obscure, combined with the potential for extraterrestrial contact, dazzles the human creative mind and fills a feeling of marvel about our spot in the universe.

All in all, the investigation of submerged secrets and UFOs addresses an outskirts of disclosure that challenges how we might interpret the world we occupy. The seas, with their secret profundities and unknown domains, hold mysteries that keep on evading us. Reports of USOs, transmedium UFOs, and submerged structures push the limits of our insight and power us to rethink the idea of our connections with the Earth and the universe.

As innovation propels and our ability for investigation develops, almost certainly, we will reveal more hints to the secrets that lie underneath the waves. The convergence of submerged secrets and UFO experiences welcomes us to move toward these peculiarities with a receptive outlook,

offsetting logical request with an acknowledgment of the boundlessness of the unexplored world. Whether the responses lie in the profundities of the seas or past the stars, the quest for understanding drives us to investigate the outskirts of our insight and embrace the secrets that characterize our reality.

6.1 Investigation of reported underwater UFO sightings and encounters.

The examination of detailed submerged UFO sightings and experiences addresses a complicated and charming area of study that mixes components of science, innovation, and the unexplained. As sightings of unidentified flying items (UFOs) keep on catching public consideration, there is a developing consciousness of occurrences that include these strange art interfacing with the World's seas. The investigation of this peculiarity requires a multidisciplinary approach, including oceanography, astronomy, and the assessment of onlooker accounts.

One of the difficulties in examining submerged UFO experiences is the innate trouble of investigating the profundities of the seas. The limitlessness of the submerged world, combined with the restrictions of current innovation, makes it trying to accumulate exhaustive information on these peculiarities. Subs, remotely worked vehicles (ROVs), and submerged drones have worked on our capacity to investigate the sea depths, however by far most of the submerged domain stays unknown and difficult to reach.

The revealed sightings of unidentified lowered objects (USOs) add a layer of intricacy to the examination. Witnesses, including maritime work force, business pilots, and regular folks, have portrayed experiences with objects showing uncommon conduct underneath the sea's surface. These experiences frequently include objects moving at high velocities, making quick moves, or showing qualities that resist the known abilities of human-made innovation.

Maritime experiences with USOs have been recorded in declassified military reports, adding a degree of validity to these records. At times, submarines furnished with cutting edge sonar frameworks have identified and followed submerged objects showing strange way of behaving. The capacity of these items to outsmart even the most complex submarines brings up issues about their starting point and impetus frameworks.

One outstanding occurrence happened in 2004 during the USS Nimitz UFO experience, where U.S. Naval force pilots noticed and drew in with unidentified flying articles off the shore of California.

MYSTERIES OF THE DEEP BLUE

The items, depicted as "Spasm Tac" formed, exhibited flight capacities that resisted the laws of physical science. In one occasion, a UFO was accounted for to have slipped into the sea, vanishing suddenly. The episode, upheld by declassified video film, features the nearby association between UFO sightings and the submerged domain.

In the examination of submerged UFO experiences, analysts and researchers wrestle with the test of isolating veritable unexplained peculiarities from misidentifications, fabrications, and regular peculiarities. Distrust is a vital component in the logical cycle, guaranteeing that ends depend on thorough proof and sensible thinking. In any case, the sheer volume of revealed sightings and the consistency of specific subtleties across various records warrant serious thought of the peculiarity.

Progressions in innovation have worked with the assortment of information connected with submerged UFO experiences. Further developed sonar frameworks, satellite innovation, and submerged cameras add to the social occasion of more point by point and exact data. At times, onlooker accounts are upheld by confirming proof, like radar information, sonar accounts, or visual documentation. The mix of numerous wellsprings of data improves the validity of revealed experiences.

One road of examination includes dissecting the geospatial dispersion of submerged UFO sightings and their nearness to known submerged highlights. A few specialists recommend that specific submerged structures, for example, channels, volcanic vents, or old vestiges, may act as focal points for extraterrestrial creatures or high level developments. Looking at the connection between's UFO sightings and explicit submerged areas could give bits of knowledge into the inspirations and examples of these unidentified specialty.

The investigation of submerged UFO experiences likewise meets with the more extensive area of astrobiology. The chance of extraterrestrial life visiting our planet prompts inquiries regarding the idea of these creatures and their advantage in Earth's seas. A few scholars propose that submerged conditions might offer exceptional circumstances for extraterrestrial investigation or residence. The quest for microbial life in outrageous submerged conditions on The planet, for example, aqueous vents, adds an extra layer to the examination, as researchers investigate the potential for comparative circumstances on different planets or moons.

Military associations, generally engaged with the examination of UFO sightings, assume an essential part in gathering and breaking down information connected with submerged experiences. Declassified military reports, for example, those delivered by the U.S. Branch of Guard, give a brief look into the authority affirmation of the peculiarity. The association of prepared onlookers, high level sensor frameworks, and cutting edge hardware highlights the earnestness with which these experiences are treated inside military circles.

The shame encompassing UFO research, frequently excused as pseudoscience or fear inspired notion, has impeded the methodical investigation of the peculiarity. Be that as it may, the developing acknowledgment of the requirement for logical investigation into UFOs has prompted a change in mentalities inside mainstream researchers. Associations like the Logical Alliance for UAP (Unidentified Elevated Peculiarities) Studies plan to carry a thorough logical way to deal with the examination of UFOs, incorporating those with submerged parts.

Moral contemplations additionally become possibly the most important factor in the examination of submerged UFO experiences. The potential for cutting edge extraterrestrial or obscure innovations communicating with Earth's seas brings up issues about the effect on marine life and biological systems. Dependable investigation and preservation of the seas become basic as scientists and policymakers explore the unfamiliar waters of possible contact with non-human insights.

The peculiarity of transmedium UFOs, equipped for consistently changing between the air and water, adds an extra layer of secret to the examination. Witnesses depict UFOs entering the sea and proceeding with their flight submerged with no evident disturbance to their development. This capacity challenges how we might interpret physical science and optimal design, provoking analysts to investigate the ramifications of cutting edge impetus frameworks that rise above the constraints of traditional airplane.

In the journey for replies, scientists draw motivation from the verifiable records of submerged secrets and legendary animals. The rich embroidery of sea fables, loaded up with stories of ocean beasts and incredible creatures underneath the waves, adds a social aspect to the examination. While fables might be established in creative mind and legend, some contend that it could likewise be a vault of aggregate human encounters and perceptions of unexplained peculiarities.

The submerged world, with its immeasurability and detachment, fills in as a material for the human creative mind. The secrets of the profound, whether established in legends or saw by contemporary pioneers, keep on powering our interest in the unexplored world. As innovation propels and our ability for investigation develops, the examination of submerged UFO experiences turns into an always advancing excursion into the profundities of the seas and the secrets that lie underneath.

The quest for answers reaches out past the logical domain and into mainstream society. Books, narratives, and movies investigate the crossing point of submerged secrets and UFO experiences, mixing logical request with creative hypothesis. The charm of the obscure, combined with the potential for extraterrestrial contact, dazzles the human creative mind and adds to a more extensive social discussion about the secrets that characterize our reality.

All in all, the examination of revealed submerged UFO sightings and experiences addresses a difficult and multi-layered pursuit. As innovation and investigation strategies keep on propelling, scientists are managed the cost of new chances to investigate the secrets of the profound. The cooperation between logical request, military examinations, and public commitment is fundamental in disentangling the riddle of submerged UFO experiences.

While wariness stays an indispensable part of the logical cycle, a receptive methodology is similarly significant when confronted with the intricacies of the unexplored world. The seas, with their secret profundities and unfamiliar domains, hold privileged insights that coax us to investigate and comprehend. As we explore the waters of disclosure, the examination of submerged UFO experiences welcomes us to embrace the secrets that challenge how we might interpret the world and our spot in the universe.

6.2 Examination of government and military involvement in studying unidentified underwater objects.

The assessment of government and military contribution in concentrating on unidentified submerged objects (UFOs) addresses a critical part of the more extensive investigation into unexplained peculiarities. States and military associations, frequently at the cutting edge of mechanical headways, play had a pivotal impact in examining and answering reports of unidentified items underneath the sea's surface. The investigation of unidentified lowered objects (USOs) brings up issues about public safety, mechanical abilities, and the possible ramifications of experiences with obscure substances in the profundities of the seas.

By and large, states have kept a degree of mystery in regards to their examinations concerning UFOs and related peculiarities. The Virus War period, portrayed by elevated pressures between worldwide superpowers, saw expanded military interest in unidentified aeronautical peculiarities. The apprehension about mechanical prevalence by rival countries powered endeavors over screen and comprehend offbeat elevated objects, whether saw in the skies or entering the World's seas.

One of the most notable occurrences of government contribution in UFO studies is the production of Undertaking Blue Book by the US Aviation based armed forces in 1952. The venture meant to examine UFO sightings and decide if these sightings represented any danger to public safety. While Undertaking Blue Book zeroed in basically on ethereal peculiarities, its presence featured the tactical's advantage in understanding and classifying unidentified articles.

The declassification of government archives as of late has revealed insight into the degree of military contribution in UFO examinations. The US Branch of Protection's affirmation of the High level Aviation

Danger Distinguishing proof Program (AATIP) in 2017 denoted a takeoff from the past position of minimizing the meaning of UFO research. AATIP, a mysterious drive subsidized by the Pentagon, zeroed in on concentrating on experiences with unidentified elevated peculiarities, including those that happened submerged.

The tactical's advantage in unidentified submerged objects is obvious in declassified reports that archive experiences between maritime vessels and submerged irregularities. Submarines furnished with cutting edge sonar frameworks have distinguished and followed objects showing

strange way of behaving, like fast speed increase, unexpected shifts in course, and the capacity to work at outrageous profundities. These experiences bring up issues about the idea of the articles and the likely innovative progressions past current human capacities.

One outstanding occurrence including government and military communication with submerged UFOs happened in 1971. The USS Trepang, a US Naval force submarine, purportedly experienced a huge, round object producing a greenish light nearby Iceland. The article's quick climb to the surface and resulting flight very high left the submarine's team confused. The occurrence, recorded in declassified documents, highlights the tactical's part in answering and endeavoring to grasp experiences with unidentified articles underneath the sea.

The arrival of declassified military film further underscores the reality with which the tactical treats experiences with unidentified items, both in the air and submerged. The USS Nimitz UFO experience in 2004, including U.S. Naval force pilots noticing and drawing in with unidentified flying articles off the bank of California, acquired far and wide consideration after the declassification and arrival of video film. The innovation and capacities showed by these UFOs surpassed the known execution qualities of any known human-made airplane.

As states and military associations recognize their contribution in concentrating on unidentified submerged objects, questions emerge about the inspirations driving these examinations. Public safety contemplations assume a critical part, as the expected presence of cutting edge and obscure innovations raises worries about unfamiliar enemies or likely dangers to oceanic interests. The capacity of submerged objects to outsmart submarines and work in manners conflicting with realized human-made innovation adds a component of direness to military examinations.

The convergence of government and military contribution with submerged UFOs additionally carries moral contemplations to the front. The expected effect of cutting edge extraterrestrial or obscure advancements on the World's seas brings up issues about natural and biological outcomes. Dependable investigation and protection of marine conditions become fundamental as military associations explore the intricacies of experiences with non-human insights.

Notwithstanding military examinations, knowledge organizations are in many cases engaged with surveying the public safety ramifications of unidentified submerged objects. The Focal Knowledge Organization (CIA) and other insight offices have verifiable connections to UFO examinations, with an emphasis on understanding potential dangers presented by unusual flying and submerged peculiarities. The declassification of reports connected with UFO research gives experiences into the cooperative endeavors among military and knowledge associations.

Global joint effort in the investigation of unidentified submerged objects is likewise clear, with reports from different nations depicting experiences with USOs. The Unified Realm, for instance, has declassified records specifying episodes including Illustrious Naval force submarines and

submerged inconsistencies. The worldwide idea of these experiences brings up issues about the comprehensiveness of the peculiarity and the requirement for global collaboration in understanding and answering submerged UFOs.

The contribution of military and government associations in concentrating on unidentified submerged objects doesn't exclusively spin around mechanical angles. Mental and sociocultural considers likewise come play, affecting how these associations approach and answer reports of UFO experiences. The likely effect on open discernment, public safety, and international elements adds intricacy to the dynamic cycles inside government and military circles.

Public mindfulness and interest in government and military contribution in UFO studies have filled altogether lately. The declassification and arrival of UFO-related records, alongside true explanations from military authorities recognizing the presence of unidentified elevated peculiarities, add to a changing story encompassing UFOs. The shift towards straightforwardness mirrors an acknowledgment of the public's more right than wrong to data and an affirmation of the meaning of UFO experiences.

The assessment of government and military contribution in concentrating on unidentified submerged protests likewise meets with the more extensive talk on UFO revelation. Advocates for straightforwardness contend that the declassification of UFO-related data is fundamental for figuring out the full extent of the peculiarity and cultivating public trust. The affirmation by military associations that specific UFO experiences stay unexplained difficulties the verifiable account that excuses such reports as simple misidentifications or tricks.

Established researchers' commitment with military and government examinations concerning unidentified submerged objects differs. While certain researchers approach the subject with distrust and watchfulness, others perceive the worth of military information and onlooker accounts in propelling comprehension we might interpret the peculiarity. The incorporation of logical request with military reports and declassified data adds to a more extensive assessment of submerged UFO experiences.

Mechanical headways keep on assuming a urgent part in the examination of unidentified submerged objects. Further developed sonar frameworks, submerged drones, and remotely worked vehicles (ROVs) improve our capacity to investigate the sea profundities and accumulate information on peculiar peculiarities. Cooperative endeavors between researchers, architects, and military staff add to the advancement of state of the art innovations that can catch, record, and dissect submerged UFO experiences with more noteworthy accuracy.

As the investigation of unidentified submerged objects develops, challenges continue recognizing authentic unexplained peculiarities from misidentifications, normal peculiarities, or lies. The intricacy of the submerged climate, combined with the limits of human discernment and innovation, requires a nuanced and cautious way to deal with information examination.

The advancement of normalized conventions for detailing and examining submerged UFO experiences adds to the validity and unwavering quality of the data assembled.

The assessment of government and military association in concentrating on unidentified submerged objects welcomes us to think about the more extensive ramifications of these experiences. Past the mechanical and logical perspectives, the peculiarity raises philosophical, social, and existential inquiries concerning humankind's spot in the universe. The affirmation of the obscure difficulties our assumptions and energizes a reconsideration of our relationship with the universe.

All in all, the assessment of government and military contribution in concentrating on unidentified submerged objects gives a window into the intricacies of the UFO peculiarity. Authentic mystery and the new shift toward straightforwardness highlight the meaning of military examinations concerning experiences with unidentified articles underneath the sea's surface. As mechanical progressions proceed and public interest develops, the cooperation between government, military, and mainstream researchers offers a promising road for disentangling the secrets of unidentified submerged protests and propelling comprehension we might interpret the unexplored world.

6.3 Discussion on the theories and speculations surrounding these mysterious phenomena.

The conversation on the hypotheses and hypotheses encompassing unidentified submerged objects (UFOs) and related peculiarities digs into a domain where science meets hypothesis, and creative mind interweaves with the quest for replies. As observer accounts, military reports, and declassified archives add to our comprehension, different speculations arise to make sense of the baffling experiences underneath the sea's surface.

1. **Extraterrestrial Speculation:**

    The most conspicuous and getting through hypothesis recommends that a few submerged UFOs are vehicles of extraterrestrial beginning. Defenders of the Extraterrestrial Speculation contend that the high level impetus frameworks, unpredictable moves, and supernatural attributes saw in UFO experiences outperform the capacities of human-made innovation. The immeasurability of the seas, with their secret profundities and unfamiliar domains, gives an optimal cover to extraterrestrial creatures to work undetected.

    As indicated by this hypothesis, extraterrestrial civilizations might be investigating Earth's seas for logical purposes, asset appraisal, or in any event, laying out secret bases. The capacity of UFOs to flawlessly progress between the air and water, as detailed in trans-medium UFO experiences, lines up with cutting edge extraterrestrial innovation intended for interstellar travel and investigation.

2. **Submerged Outsider Bases:**

    Expanding upon the Extraterrestrial Speculation, a few scholars guess about the presence of submerged outsider bases. The seas, covering over 70% of the World's surface, offer immense and generally neglected regions where extraterrestrial creatures could lay out disguised establishments. Reports of submerged structures and monstrous mathematical arrangements, frequently excused by cynics as regular developments, fuel hypothesis about the presence of stowed away bases underneath the waves.

    Defenders of the submerged outsider bases hypothesis highlight peculiarities, for example, the strange designs found off the shoreline of Japan and Cuba. These designs, with their mathematical accuracy and puzzling profundity, bring up issues about their starting point and reason. While standard science will in general ascribe such arrangements to regular cycles, advocates contend that the intricacy and size of these designs oppose customary clarifications.

3. **Interdimensional and Time Travel Speculations:**
An elective point of view proposes that a few unidentified submerged items might begin from aspects outside our ability to comprehend or include time travel. Advocates of interdimensional hypotheses recommend that specific UFO experiences include substances or art progressing between various aspects, making sense of their abrupt appearances and vanishings. The tremendousness and secrets of the seas might act as entries or doors for interdimensional creatures.

Time travel speculations set that cutting-edge developments, whether extraterrestrial or earthly, have the ability to control time. The idea of submerged create working across various fleeting real factors acquaints a speculative component with the examination. While these speculations stretch the limits of momentum logical comprehension, they resound with the intrinsic secret of UFO experiences and the unfamiliar regions of the seas.

4. **Secret Military Undertakings:**
A more grounded yet similarly charming hypothesis proposes that a few unidentified submerged items might be ordered military ventures created by world states. Defenders of this hypothesis contend that exceptional impetus frameworks, secrecy abilities, and transmedium capacities showed by specific UFOs line up with the qualities of profoundly ordered military advances. These ventures could include unpredictable aeronautical and submerged vehicles intended for observation, surveillance, or even essential guard purposes.

The military's verifiable contribution in UFO examinations, as exemplified by projects like AATIP, adds weight to the possibility that a few submerged UFOs might be the consequence of mystery military drives. The subtle pretense encompassing grouped projects adds to the trouble in recognizing unpredictable military innovation and really unexplained peculiarities.

5. **Natural Peculiarities and Normal Clarifications:**
   Cynics and standard researchers frequently incline towards regular clarifications for announced submerged UFO experiences. Natural peculiarities, like bioluminescent life forms, submerged geothermal movement, and normal methane hydrate ejections, are proposed as expected wellsprings of misidentification. The limitlessness and intricacy of the seas make conditions where new regular peculiarities can show, driving eyewitnesses to decipher them as bizarre.

   While this point of view tries to ground clarifications in known logical standards, it may not completely represent the consistency of specific UFO attributes announced across assorted experiences. Witnesses frequently depict objects displaying controlled, insightful way of behaving, which is trying to accommodate with simply normal peculiarities.

6. **Mental and Perceptual Elements:**
   Mental and perceptual variables add to the intricacy of understanding and deciphering UFO experiences. Mental predispositions, optical deceptions, and the impact of social stories about UFOs can shape how people see and review their encounters. The immense, dull fields of the sea can enhance perceptual difficulties, prompting misinterpretations of standard peculiarities.

   The mental clarification doesn't excuse the veritable idea of witnesses' encounters yet rather accentuates the job of human discernment in molding those encounters. Mental variables, joined with the secretive idea of the submerged climate, add to the rich woven artwork of UFO experiences and the trouble in showing up at authoritative clarifications.

7. **Flighty Earthly Innovations:**
   Notwithstanding secret military activities, a few speculations propose the inclusion of whimsical earthbound innovations created by confidential substances or examination associations. Defenders of this hypothesis recommend that forward leaps in impetus, energy, or materials science could prompt the formation of capricious vehicles equipped for transmedium travel. Such advances, if in the possession of private elements, could work outside the domain of government exposure.

   The journey for clean energy and imaginative impetus frameworks has prodded examination into colorful innovations that challenge ordinary comprehension. The chance of forward leaps in repulsive force or electromagnetic impetus, while speculative, lines up with the possibility that a few unidentified submerged items could be the consequence of earthbound trial and error.

8. **Social and Folkloric Impacts:**
   The impact of social stories, legends, and folklore adds a layer of intricacy to the understanding of UFO experiences. From the beginning of time, different societies have woven stories of submerged substances, ocean beasts, and legendary creatures dwelling in the profundities. The model symbolism of strange animals underneath the waves might impact how witnesses decipher and portray their encounters.

   The social and folkloric impacts hypothesis proposes that the human brain, affected by aggregate legends and stories, may decipher obscure peculiarities from the perspective of natural accounts. While this point of view doesn't limit the truth of UFO experiences, it features the job of social molding in forming discernments.

9. **Mixture Hypotheses**
   Given the complex idea of unidentified submerged articles and UFO experiences, a few scientists propose half breed hypotheses that consolidate components of various clarifications. For

instance, a half breed hypothesis could propose that specific experiences include both characterized military undertakings and certifiable unidentified peculiarities. The transaction between normal peculiarities, cutting edge innovations, and social impacts could add to the intricacy of individual cases.

Half and half speculations perceive the different variables at play in the UFO peculiarity and try to integrate different components into a more complete structure. The test lies in knowing the particular commitments of each figure explicit cases.

Amidst these hypotheses and theories, recognizing the constraints of our ongoing information and the requirement for proceeded with investigation and inquiry is fundamental. The secrets of unidentified submerged objects continue, powered by the endlessness of the seas and the puzzling idea of experiences revealed by observers all over the planet.

As mechanical headways open new outskirts in sea investigation and our comprehension of physical science and impetus develops, the talk encompassing submerged UFOs will probably keep on advancing. Logical request, combined with a receptiveness to capricious potential outcomes, will assume a urgent part in unwinding the secrets that lie underneath the sea's surface and past the ranges of our momentum understanding. The conversation on hypotheses and theories fills in as a unique investigation of the obscure, welcoming us to ponder the remarkable potential outcomes that might prowl in the profound waters of our planet.

The hypotheses encompassing baffling peculiarities, especially those including unidentified items underneath the sea's surface, are a kaleidoscope of speculations that mix science, creative mind, and the unexplained. As reports of unidentified submerged objects (UFOs) keep on catching public consideration, a different scope of theories arises, offering different focal points through which to decipher these confounding experiences.

1. **Extraterrestrial Guests:**
   One of the most persevering and well known hypotheses is established in the possibility that a few submerged UFOs are vehicles of extraterrestrial beginning. Advocates of this hypothesis set that the high level capacities, flighty developments, and transmedium travel showed by specific UFOs outperform the constraints of human innovation.
   The immeasurability of the seas gives a characteristic disguise to extraterrestrial creatures leading investigation, research, or furtive exercises.
   As per this hypothesis, extraterrestrial human advancements might find Earth's seas favorable for covert tasks, utilizing the water's haziness to stay stowed away from earthly spectators. The expected presence of submerged extraterrestrial bases adds a layer of interest to this hypothesis, recommending that the profundities of the seas might hold onto covered establishments where supernatural insights lead their issues past the range of human identification.

2. **Interdimensional Substances:**
   Hypotheses including interdimensional substances present the possibility that a few unidentified submerged items might begin from aspects past our regular comprehension. Defenders of this hypothesis recommend that specific UFO experiences include substances or art progressing between various aspects, making sense of their sudden appearances and vanishings. The immensity and secrets of the seas, in this specific circumstance, could act as entryways or doors through which interdimensional creatures navigate.
   This speculative system challenges conventional thoughts of the real world and places that the baffling experiences might be looks into equal aspects or substitute real factors. While solidly established in the domain of hypothetical

material science, the interdimensional hypothesis adds a layer of intricacy to the examination of submerged UFOs.

3. **Time Travel and Worldly Peculiarities:**
   Expanding on the idea of interdimensional travel, a few hypotheses engage the likelihood that submerged UFOs include time travel or control of worldly real factors. The thought is that cutting-edge developments, whether extraterrestrial or future emphasess of mankind, have the innovative ability to explore through time. Experiences with submerged UFOs may, as per this hypothesis, address occasions where people who goes back and forth through time or transiently dislodged objects collaborate with our present.

   While immovably arranged in the domain of speculative sci-fi, the idea of time-traveling UFOs adds a component of interest to the secrets of the sea. The unknown profundities become a likely jungle gym for substances existing external the limitations of direct time.

4. **Submerged Civilizations:**
   Hypotheses about submerged civilizations propose the presence of cutting edge creatures or keen elements dwelling in the profundities of Earth's seas. This hypothesis recommends that these submerged civic establishments, perhaps obscure to surface-staying humankind, have advancements that manifest as unidentified articles when experienced.

   The strange designs found off the shores of Japan and Cuba, frequently refered to as likely proof, add to the hypothesis about old or outsider submerged social orders.

   The chance of unseen civic establishments existing in Earth's seas takes advantage of the charm of investigation and disclosure. It welcomes us to envision a world underneath the waves overflowing with shrewd lifeforms that have figured out how to evade our comprehension.

5. **Secret Military Advances:**
A more grounded at this point similarly charming hypothesis rotates around the contribution of mystery military advancements in the making of unidentified submerged objects. Defenders of this hypothesis recommend that specific experiences might be the aftereffect of characterized military activities, including progressed drive frameworks, secrecy abilities, and transmedium innovations. The military's authentic job in UFO examinations, as exemplified by projects like AATIP, energizes hypothesis about the presence of whimsical ethereal and submerged vehicles.

The smoke screen encompassing military tasks and examination projects adds to the trouble in recognizing authentic unidentified peculiarities and human-made advances. Hypotheses including secret military innovations help us to remember the obscured lines between logical progression and the unexplored world.

6. **Maritime Abnormalities and Regular Peculiarities:**
A more doubtful viewpoint thinks about how conceivable it is that many revealed submerged UFO experiences might have normal clarifications established in Natural peculiarities. Bioluminescent life forms, submerged geothermal action, and methane hydrate emissions are among the normal events that doubters highlight as expected wellsprings of misidentification. The tremendousness and intricacy of the seas establish a climate where new regular peculiarities can show, driving spectators to decipher them as bizarre.

While this speculative structure tries to ground clarifications in known logical standards, it may not completely represent the consistency of specific UFO qualities revealed across different experiences. Witnesses frequently portray objects showing controlled, wise way of behaving, testing a direct excusal of these encounters as simple misidentifications.

7. **Mental and Insight Based Clarifications:**
Hypotheses including mental and perceptual elements perceive the job of human discernment in forming UFO experiences. Mental inclinations, optical deceptions, and the impact of social accounts about UFOs can add to the understanding and review of encounters. The huge, dim spans of the sea might intensify perceptual difficulties, prompting misinterpretations of conventional peculiarities.

This speculative focal point stresses the abstract idea of UFO experiences, where individual and aggregate discernments shape the stories. While not limiting the realness of witnesses' encounters, the mental and perceptual viewpoint empowers a nuanced investigation of the human brain's job in molding understandings.

8. **Crossover Hypotheses:**
Given the multi-layered nature of unidentified submerged articles and UFO experiences, a few examiners propose cross breed speculations that consolidate components of numerous clarifications. For example, a half and half hypothesis could propose that specific experiences include a mix of normal peculiarities, ordered military innovations, and truly unexplained events. The exchange between different variables could add to the intricacy and variety of individual cases.

Cross breed hypotheses mirror an affirmation of the assorted variables at play in the UFO peculiarity. While testing to parse out the particular commitments of each calculate explicit cases, mixture hypotheses look to offer a more extensive system for understanding the intricacies in question.

9. Social and Folkloric Impacts:

The impact of social stories, fables, and folklore acquaints one more layer with the hypotheses encompassing unidentified submerged objects. Since forever ago, different societies have woven stories of submerged elements, ocean beasts, and legendary creatures living in the profundities. Advocates of this hypothesis contend that the human psyche, impacted by aggregate legends and stories, may decipher obscure peculiarities from the perspective of recognizable accounts.

This speculative system empowers an investigation of how social molding and prototype symbolism add to the forming of UFO experiences. While not giving a conclusive clarification, the social and folkloric impacts hypothesis features the harmonious connection between human creative mind and the secrets of the profound.

In the embroidery of hypotheses encompassing baffling submerged peculiarities, every hypothesis offers a remarkable viewpoint that would be useful. The investigation of these hypotheses fills in as a dynamic and developing investigation into the obscure, welcoming us to examine the phenomenal potential outcomes that might be sneaking in the profundities of our planet's seas. As innovation propels, how we might interpret the universe extends, and the limits of human information are pushed at any point further, the conversation on these hypotheses stays a fundamental piece of the continuous mission to unwind the secrets of unidentified submerged objects.

Chapter 7

"The Future of Deep-Sea Exploration"

The fate of remote ocean investigation holds monstrous commitment and potential, driven by mechanical headways and a developing comprehension of the significance of the profound sea climate. As we dig into the 21st 100 years, the investigation of the remote ocean has turned into a point of convergence for logical request, natural observing, asset extraction, and, surprisingly, possible residence. This immense and puzzling domain, covering the greater part of the World's surface, has for quite some time been a wellspring of interest and interest, at this point its profundities remain generally neglected and unknown.

One of the critical drivers representing things to come of remote ocean investigation is the improvement of state of the art advancements that empower researchers and scientists to arrive at exceptional profundities and assemble important information. Conventional strategies for remote ocean investigation, like monitored submarines and remotely worked vehicles (ROVs), have been fundamental in giving looks into the pit. Be that as it may, these strategies have constraints, including significant expenses, restricted versatility, and the failure to arrive at outrageous profundities.

The coming of independent submerged vehicles (AUVs) has reformed remote ocean investigation by offering a practical and proficient method for social event information from the sea's profundities. These automated vehicles are outfitted with modern sensors and instruments that can catch high-goal pictures, gather tests, and measure different natural boundaries. AUVs are fit for directing reviews over enormous regions, giving a more exhaustive comprehension of remote ocean environments and land highlights.

Besides, progressions in advanced mechanics and man-made reasoning (computer based intelligence) have prompted the improvement of savvy submerged drones that can explore independently through testing territories. These robots can adjust to evolving conditions, stay away from deterrents, and enhance their courses, considering more exact and designated investigation. The joining of simulated intelligence into remote ocean investigation upgrades the capacities of automated frameworks as well as works with continuous information examination, empowering researchers to pursue informed choices during investigation missions.

Notwithstanding mechanical developments, worldwide coordinated effort assumes an essential part coming soon for remote ocean investigation. The profound sea is a worldwide asset that rises above public boundaries, and a cooperative methodology is fundamental for boosting the advantages of investigation and tending to shared difficulties. The Unified Countries Show on the Law of the Ocean (UNCLOS) gives a structure to the reasonable utilization of the seas and advances participation in sea life logical examination.

Cooperative drives, for example, the Nippon Establishment GEBCO Seabed 2030 Task, intend to plan the whole sea depths constantly 2030. This aggressive endeavor includes an organization of worldwide accomplices cooperating to incorporate and share bathymetric information, making a thorough guide of the ocean bottom. Precise planning of the sea depths is essential to grasping marine geography, recognizing expected mineral assets, and arranging future investigation missions.

As remote ocean investigation advances, there is a developing acknowledgment of the natural meaning of the profound sea and the requirement for preservation measures. Remote ocean environments are home to a different exhibit of animal groups, a large number of which are adjusted to outrageous circumstances, like high tension, low temperatures, and complete murkiness. These exceptional environments have living beings with novel biochemical mixtures that have the potential for drug and biotechnological applications.

Be that as it may, remote ocean environments are additionally helpless against human exercises, including remote ocean mining, base fishing, and contamination. The Worldwide Seabed Authority (ISA) manages remote ocean mining exercises in global waters, planning to adjust the financial interests of mining with the need to safeguard the marine climate.

Preservation endeavors are vital for protect the biodiversity of the profound sea and forestall irreversible harm to these fragile biological systems.

The investigation of aqueous vents, cold leaks, and other remote ocean living spaces has uncovered an abundance of organic and topographical disclosures. Aqueous vents, specifically, are focal points of biodiversity, supporting exceptional networks of organic entities that flourish without a trace of daylight. These biological systems depend on chemosynthetic microbes that convert synthetics from the vent liquid into energy, framing the premise of the food web in these outrageous conditions.

Understanding the interconnectedness of remote ocean biological systems is critical for viable protection techniques. The Show on Natural Variety (CBD) perceives the significance of protecting marine biodiversity and stresses the requirement for the practical utilization of marine assets. As remote ocean investigation progresses, it is basic to figure out some kind of harmony between saddling the capability of the profound sea and protecting its delicate environments.

The eventual fate of remote ocean investigation reaches out past logical request and protection to include the potential for asset extraction. The profound sea harbors significant minerals and metals, including polymetallic knobs, polymetallic sulfides, and cobalt-rich ferromanganese outsides. These assets have drawn in interest from businesses looking to profit by the monetary open doors introduced by remote ocean mining.

Nonetheless, the possibility of remote ocean mining raises worries about its natural effect and the potential for hopeless mischief to remote ocean environments. The fragile harmony between monetary turn of events and ecological preservation requires cautious thought and the foundation of hearty administrative structures. The ISA, through its job in controlling mineral-related exercises in the global seabed region, assumes a critical part in molding the eventual fate of remote ocean mining.

The improvement of reasonable practices and innovations is fundamental to relieve the natural effect of remote ocean mining. Analysts and industry partners are investigating creative arrangements, for example, low-influence mining methods, to limit aggravations to the ocean bottom. Moreover, the recovery and reusing of metals from electronic waste and earthbound mines add to diminishing the interest for remote ocean assets.

The potential for remote ocean investigation goes past logical disclosure and asset extraction to incorporate the chance of submerged residence and framework. As the worldwide populace keeps on developing, there is expanding interest in investigating new outskirts for human settlement, and the profound sea presents a special open door. The improvement of submerged territories and subsea framework could give answers for difficulties like overpopulation, land shortage, and ecological maintainability.

The idea of submerged territories, frequently alluded to as "aquanautics," includes the making of independent networks underneath the sea's surface. These territories would have to address basic factors like life emotionally supportive networks, energy age, squander the board, and mental prosperity. Specialists are investigating the potential for secluded and expandable submerged structures that can oblige human necessities while limiting the ecological effect on the encompassing environments.

Headways in materials science, designing, and biotechnology add to the plausibility of submerged residence. The utilization of cutting edge materials, like carbon composites and straightforward polymers, takes into consideration the development of tough and versatile submerged structures. Biotechnological developments, for example, shut circle aquaponic frameworks, empower the development of food inside submerged living spaces, diminishing reliance on outer assets.

The foundation of submerged natural surroundings likewise raises moral and legitimate contemplations. The Space Deal, which oversees human exercises in space, fills in as a point of reference for resolving legitimate issues connected with submerged home. The worldwide local area should work cooperatively to foster a legitimate structure that guarantees the dependable and feasible utilization of the profound sea for human settlement while saving its natural respectability.

All in all, the eventual fate of remote ocean investigation holds tremendous potential outcomes, driven by mechanical progressions, worldwide cooperation, and a developing familiarity with the significance of the profound sea climate. From the improvement of independent submerged vehicles and clever submerged robots to cooperative drives for exhaustive sea planning, the devices and systems for investigating the remote ocean are turning out to be more complex and successful.

As investigation advances, there is a squeezing need to adjust logical disclosure, asset extraction, and natural protection. The sensitive biological systems of the profound sea, with their extraordinary biodiversity and potential for drug applications, should be defended against the effects of human exercises like remote ocean mining. Worldwide associations, including the Assembled Countries, the Global Seabed

Authority, and the Show on Organic Variety, assume essential parts in forming the administrative structures and preservation endeavors that will characterize the eventual fate of remote ocean investigation.

Besides, the potential for submerged residence acquaints another aspect with the investigation of the profound sea. As mankind seeks the seas for answers for difficulties, for example, overpopulation and ecological supportability, the advancement of submerged living spaces requires cautious thought of specialized, moral, and lawful perspectives.

The next few decades are probably going to observe further leap forwards in remote ocean investigation, offering uncommon bits of knowledge into the secrets of the pit and preparing for capable and practical utilization of this tremendous and neglected outskirts.

7.1 Overview of cutting-edge technologies used in deep-sea exploration.

Remote ocean investigation has entered another time portrayed by the arrangement of state of the art advances that have extended our capacity to study and grasp the secrets of the sea profundities. These headways length different disciplines, going from advanced mechanics and man-made brainpower to materials science and remote detecting. As we leave on this excursion to investigate the most un-saw part of our planet, these advancements assume a urgent part in defeating the difficulties related with outrageous circumstances, enormous tensions, and restricted openness.

One of the key mechanical advancements driving remote ocean investigation is the turn of events and arrangement of independent submerged vehicles (AUVs). AUVs are untethered, battery-controlled vehicles outfitted with a set-up of sensors and instruments that empower them to independently explore and gather information. In contrast to customary remotely worked vehicles (ROVs) that require a surface association, AUVs work freely, offering more noteworthy adaptability and effectiveness in investigating tremendous region of the profound sea.

These vehicles are intended to endure the cruel states of the remote ocean, including outrageous strain, low temperatures, and complete obscurity. They are outfitted with cutting edge route frameworks, permitting them to follow predefined directions or adjust to changing circumstances continuously. The sensors on AUVs catch high-goal pictures, map the ocean bottom, measure water properties, and gather tests, furnishing researchers with important information for land, organic, and natural examinations.

Notwithstanding AUVs, remotely worked vehicles (ROVs) keep on assuming a vital part in remote ocean investigation. ROVs are associated with the surface by a link, which supplies power and takes into consideration constant correspondence. This fastened association gives more noteworthy control and mobility, making ROVs reasonable for unpredictable undertakings like example assortment, hardware control, and mediation in submerged tasks.

Current ROVs are furnished with top quality cameras, controller arms, and a scope of specific devices, permitting scientists to direct definite and exact work in the profound sea. These vehicles are in many cases utilized related to AUVs to lead exhaustive investigation missions, consolidating the independence of AUVs with the ongoing control and control abilities of ROVs.

Progressions in mechanical technology have additionally brought about astute submerged drones that can explore independently through testing conditions. These robots are outfitted with sensors and cameras, and they influence man-made brainpower (artificial intelligence) calculations to dissect information and pursue choices continuously. Shrewd robots can adjust to evolving conditions, stay away from impediments, and improve their ways, giving a more effective and designated way to deal with remote ocean investigation.

The combination of simulated intelligence into remote ocean investigation stretches out past insightful robots. AI calculations are utilized in information examination to recognize designs, characterize species, and concentrate significant data from huge datasets. This capacity improves the productivity of logical examination via computerizing undertakings that would be tedious for human administrators. Artificial intelligence additionally adds to the advancement of prescient models for oceanographic peculiarities and aids continuous decision-production during investigation missions.

Satellite innovation assumes a critical part in remote detecting and observing of the seas. While satellites basically notice the outer layer of the sea, they give important data on ocean surface temperature, sea flows, and, surprisingly, the discovery of phytoplankton sprouts. This information is instrumental in understanding the unique cycles happening in the upper layers of the sea and adds to the general comprehension of sea flow examples and environment related changes.

Lately, headways in satellite innovation have stretched out our observational abilities to incorporate subsurface elements. Satellite altimetry, for instance, can be utilized to distinguish varieties in the ocean surface level, uncovering the presence of submerged mountains and other geological elements. These perceptions are fundamental for planning the ocean bottom and arranging remote ocean investigation missions.

Submerged acoustics is one more basic innovation in remote ocean investigation. Sound waves can travel significant distances in water, permitting specialists to utilize sonar frameworks to plan the ocean bottom, find submerged highlights, and study marine life. Side-filter sonar and multibeam sonar frameworks give high-goal pictures of the ocean bottom, assisting researchers with recognizing topographical developments, for example, aqueous vents and undersea volcanoes.

Moreover, progresses in imaging innovation have empowered researchers to catch shocking superior quality pictures and recordings of the remote ocean climate. High-goal cameras on AUVs, ROVs, and clever robots give nitty gritty visuals of submerged scenes and the assorted marine life that possesses these outrageous conditions. This visual information upgrades how we might interpret remote ocean environments and helps in the recognizable proof of new species.

In the domain of materials science, the advancement of hearty and versatile materials is significant for enduring the outrageous states of the profound sea. Submerged vehicles and gear should be intended to persevere through high strain, destructive saltwater, and low temperatures. The utilization of cutting edge materials, for example, carbon composites and titanium combinations, guarantees the primary respectability of remote ocean vehicles and instruments.

One of the prominent difficulties in remote ocean investigation is the capacity to send information from the sea profundities to the surface. Customary techniques, like long links, have restrictions as far as information move rates and defenselessness to harm. Arising advances, including acoustic modems and submerged correspondence organizations, plan to address this test by empowering quicker and more solid information transmission continuously.

Remote ocean investigation isn't just about mechanical progressions yet in addition about worldwide cooperation. The intricacy of the sea climate, combined with the requirement for assorted ability, has prompted cooperative drives including researchers, designers, and associations from around the world. The Nippon Establishment GEBCO Seabed 2030 Task, for instance, is a cooperative work to plan the whole sea floor continuously 2030, depending on commitments from a worldwide organization of accomplices.

The Unified Countries Show on the Law of the Ocean (UNCLOS) gives a legitimate structure to the investigation and utilization of the seas. UNCLOS lays out the limitations of countries regarding the seabed, the water section, and the marine climate. The Worldwide Seabed Authority (ISA), laid out under UNCLOS, controls mineral-related exercises in the global seabed region to guarantee the mindful utilization of remote ocean assets.

As remote ocean investigation advances, moral contemplations come to the very front. The potential for asset extraction, especially through remote ocean mining, brings up issues about the natural effect and the impartial dissemination of advantages. Finding some kind of harmony between monetary turn of events and natural preservation requires cautious thought of moral standards and the foundation of straightforward and responsible administrative systems.

Protection endeavors are foremost despite expanding human exercises in the profound sea. Remote ocean environments, with their remarkable biodiversity and biological importance, are helpless against unsettling influences from mining, fishing, and contamination. The Show on Organic Variety (CBD) underscores the significance of saving marine biodiversity and requires the maintainable administration of marine assets.

Aqueous vents and cold leaks, found through remote ocean investigation, are environments specifically compelling because of their remarkable organic networks and land highlights. These conditions, described by outrageous circumstances and the presence of chemosynthetic organic entities, can possibly yield important experiences into the starting points of life on The planet and the potential outcomes of life on different planets.

The improvement of manageable practices is fundamental to alleviate the natural effect of remote ocean exercises, including mining. Analysts and industry partners are investigating creative arrangements, for example, low-influence mining strategies, to limit aggravations to the ocean bottom. Also, the reusing of metals from electronic waste and earthbound mines can add to diminishing the interest for remote ocean assets.

The potential for submerged residence and framework acquaints another aspect with the fate of remote ocean investigation. As the worldwide populace develops, and worries about overpopulation, land shortage, and natural manageability strengthen, the profound sea presents a special chance for human settlement. The improvement of submerged living spaces and subsea framework requires interdisciplinary cooperation, including fields like design, designing, science, and brain research.

The idea of submerged living spaces includes the production of independent networks underneath the sea's surface. These living spaces should address difficulties like life emotionally supportive networks, energy age, squander the executives, and mental prosperity. Measured and expandable designs are imagined to oblige the different necessities of submerged occupants while limiting the ecological effect on the encompassing environments.

Materials science and designing progressions are vital in the plan and development of submerged living spaces. The utilization of straightforward polymers and high level composites takes into consideration the production of sturdy and tough designs equipped for enduring the tensions of the profound sea. Biotechnological advancements, for example, shut circle aquaponic frameworks, empower the development of food inside submerged natural surroundings, adding to the supportability of these networks.

Be that as it may, the foundation of submerged living spaces raises moral and lawful contemplations. The Space Settlement, which oversees human exercises in space, fills in as a point of reference for resolving lawful issues connected with submerged residence. The global local area should work cooperatively to foster a legitimate structure that guarantees the capable and maintainable utilization of the profound sea for human settlement while saving its environmental uprightness.

All in all, the outline of state of the art advances utilized in remote ocean investigation highlights the noteworthy headway made in our capacity to study and figure out the profound sea. From independent submerged vehicles and remotely worked vehicles to wise submerged drones and high level imaging innovation, these advancements have extended the conceivable outcomes of investigation and opened new wildernesses for logical revelation, asset extraction, and possible human home.

As we adventure into the unfamiliar profundities of the sea, embracing an all encompassing and dependable approach is fundamental. Worldwide coordinated effort, directed by legitimate structures, for example, UNCLOS and the ISA, assumes an essential part in guaranteeing the manageable utilization of remote ocean assets. Moral contemplations should be at the very front of direction, especially with regards to asset extraction and the likely foundation of submerged territories.

The fate of remote ocean investigation holds extraordinary commitment, and the proceeded with advancement of state of the art advances will be instrumental in opening the mysteries of the sea profundities. As we explore the difficulties and open doors introduced by the remote ocean, the cooperative endeavors of researchers, designers, policymakers, and the global local area will shape the direction of investigation and decide how we capably and economically connect with this tremendous and strange boondocks.

7.2 Discussion on ongoing research and the potential for new discoveries.

Continuous examination in remote ocean investigation is pushing the limits of how we might interpret this tremendous and puzzling climate, uncovering new bits of knowledge into the topographical, organic, and substance processes that shape the profound sea. As innovation keeps on propelling, researchers are ready to make momentous disclosures that could have significant ramifications for how we might interpret life on The planet, the beginnings of the planet, and the potential for extraterrestrial life.

One area of progressing research centers around the investigation of outrageous conditions in the remote ocean, for example, aqueous vents and cold leaks. These one of a kind environments, described by high tensions, outrageous temperatures, and the shortfall of daylight, have an assortment of life shapes that have adjusted to these unforgiving circumstances. Researchers are leading top to bottom examinations to disentangle the mysteries of these environments, investigating the biodiversity, biological elements, and transformative cycles that oversee life in the profound.

Aqueous vents, specifically, are known for supporting flourishing networks of organic entities that depend on chemosynthetic microorganisms for their energy. These microbes convert synthetic substances from the vent liquid into natural matter, shaping the premise of the food web in these remote ocean biological systems.

Continuous exploration tries to grasp the connections between various species in these networks, as well as the components that permit life to prosper without daylight.

Notwithstanding natural examinations, analysts are researching the mineral assets related with aqueous vents. These vents are much of the time locales of extraordinary mineral statement, bringing about the development of polymetallic sulfides that contain significant metals like copper, zinc, and gold. The potential for remote ocean mining here has prompted worries about the ecological effect on these delicate environments. Progressing research means to survey the natural results of mining exercises and foster supportable practices to limit hurt.

Cold leaks, one more interesting remote ocean climate, are described by the sluggish arrival of methane and different hydrocarbons from the ocean bottom. These leaks support special networks of creatures adjusted to the low temperatures and high tensions of the profound sea. Progressing research is disentangling the natural collaborations inside cold leak biological systems and exploring the job of methane in supporting life in these conditions.

Headways in imaging innovation, remembering superior quality cameras for AUVs and ROVs, have empowered researchers to catch definite pictures and recordings of remote ocean life. These visuals give phenomenal experiences into the ways of behaving, transformations, and collaborations of species right at home. Progressing research endeavors influence these imaging capacities to report new species, concentrate on creature ways of behaving, and screen changes in remote ocean environments over the long haul.

Past natural investigation, continuous examination is digging into the geographical cycles that shape the ocean bottom and the designs tracked down in the profound sea. Planning the geography of the sea depths is a basic part of this examination, and drives like the Nippon Establishment GEBCO Seabed 2030 Undertaking intend to make an exhaustive guide of the whole ocean bottom. Exact bathymetric information is fundamental for figuring out structural cycles, recognizing likely mineral assets, and arranging future investigation missions.

The investigation of ocean bottom topography additionally includes exploring undersea volcanoes and aqueous vent frameworks. These powerful land highlights assume a critical part in molding the ocean bottom and impacting the synthetic creation of the sea. Continuous exploration looks to disentangle the cycles driving submerged volcanic action, the development of mineral stores, and their effect on the general climate.

Research vessels furnished with cutting edge sonar frameworks contribute altogether to how we might interpret ocean bottom geography. Side-filter sonar and multibeam sonar give nitty gritty pictures of the ocean bottom, permitting researchers to recognize geographical developments, map submerged scenes, and find areas of interest for additional investigation.

These apparatuses are essential for arranging designated research missions and advancing the organization of AUVs and ROVs.

One more area of progressing research includes the investigation of remote ocean silt and their part in carbon sequestration. The profound sea goes about as a critical sink for carbon dioxide, with natural particles sinking from the surface and gathering on the ocean bottom. Understanding the cycles that administer carbon entombment in remote ocean residue is fundamental for demonstrating worldwide carbon cycles and evaluating the expected effect of environmental change on carbon sequestration in the profound sea.

Microbial life in remote ocean dregs is likewise a focal point of continuous examination. Notwithstanding the difficult circumstances, microorganisms flourish in the subsurface residue, assuming a pivotal part in biogeochemical cycles. Progressing concentrates on plan to portray the variety of remote ocean organisms, investigate their metabolic cycles, and grasp their commitments to supplement cycling and carbon remineralization.

Progressions in genomic advances have worked with the investigation of microbial networks in the remote ocean. Metagenomic approaches permit researchers to break down the aggregate hereditary material of whole microbial networks, giving bits of knowledge into their utilitarian capacities and possible variations to outrageous circumstances. Progressing research in remote ocean microbial science adds to our more extensive comprehension of life's versatility and strength in outrageous conditions.

The potential for new revelations in the remote ocean reaches out to the domain of marine biotechnology. Remote ocean living beings have advanced special biochemical mixtures and atomic transformations in light of the outrageous states of the profound sea. Continuous examination investigates the biotechnological capability of these mixtures for applications in medication, industry, and natural checking.

Catalysts, proteins, and other bioactive mixtures got from remote ocean organic entities have shown guarantee in different fields, including drugs, bioremediation, and the improvement of novel materials. Progressing bioprospecting endeavors expect to recognize and describe these significant mixtures, opening the potential for new medications, biomaterials, and biotechnological developments.

The investigation of the remote ocean additionally adds to how we might interpret Earth's set of experiences and the potential for life past our planet. The outrageous circumstances tracked down in the profound sea, including high strain, low temperatures, and restricted daylight, act as analogs for conditions on other divine bodies, like frosty moons and exoplanets. Continuous examination researches the restrictions of life on The planet and the expected livability of extraterrestrial conditions.

Subsurface sea universes, for example, the subsurface expanses of moons like Europa and Enceladus, present charming opportunities for the presence of life past Earth. Continuous examination endeavors look to grasp the likely tenability of these subsurface seas, investigating the circumstances that could uphold microbial life and the possibilities for future investigation missions to these far off divine bodies.

As we dive further into the secrets of the remote ocean, progressing research is growing our insight into the interconnectedness between Earth's geosphere, hydrosphere, and biosphere. The revelations made in the profound sea have suggestions for how we might interpret planetary cycles, the development of life on The planet, and the potential for life somewhere else in the universe.

All in all, continuous examination in remote ocean investigation is a dynamic and complex undertaking that traverses organic, topographical, substance, and mechanical disciplines. The utilization of state of the art innovations, from AUVs and ROVs to cutting edge imaging and genomic apparatuses, is changing our capacity to study and report the profound sea. The potential for new revelations in aqueous vents, cold leaks, ocean bottom geography, and microbial life opens roads for propelling comprehension we might interpret Earth's set of experiences, the beginnings of life, and the opportunities for extraterrestrial livability. As researchers keep on pushing the limits of investigation, the remote ocean stays a boondocks of disclosure and a wellspring of motivation for unwinding the secrets of our planet and the more extensive universe.

7.3 Reflection on the importance of preserving the mysteries of the deep blue for future generations.

Considering the significance of protecting the secrets of the dark blue for people in the future urges us to perceive the significant meaning of the sea in molding the World's environment, supporting different biological systems, and moving a feeling of marvel and investigation. As we stand at the junction of propelling innovation and expanding human exercises in the profound sea, it becomes basic to consider the drawn out results of our activities and the moral obligation we bear to defend the secrets that lie underneath the waves.

The dark blue, addressing the tremendous spread of the world's seas, assumes a urgent part in controlling the planet's environment. Seas go about as the World's essential intensity supply, retaining and rearranging sun based energy. The sea's flows, driven by wind examples and temperature angles, impact atmospheric conditions and add to the general steadiness of the worldwide environment. Perceiving the interconnectedness of the sea and the climate highlights the significance of safeguarding the uprightness of the dark blue for people in the future.

Moreover, the sea is a basic part of the carbon cycle, filling in as a sink for carbon dioxide. Phytoplankton, minuscule marine plants, perform photosynthesis and ingest carbon dioxide from the air. As a feature of the marine food web, phytoplankton upholds the whole sea environment and assumes a vital part in sequestering carbon. Safeguarding the secrets of the dark blue is inseparable from guaranteeing the strength of marine biological systems and their capacity to alleviate environmental change by catching and putting away carbon.

The mind boggling biodiversity found in the profound sea is a demonstration of the flexibility and versatility of life on The planet. From the peculiar animals staying close aqueous vents to the tricky species possessing the haziest profundities, the dark blue harbors an abundance of life shapes that have developed to flourish in outrageous circumstances. Safeguarding these secrets isn't simply a demonstration of protection; it is a guarantee to keeping up with the multifaceted trap of life that supports the sea and, thusly, upholds life ashore.

The moral basic to safeguard the secrets of the dark blue is grounded in the comprehension that the sea is a common worldwide asset. As mankind faces squeezing difficulties, for example, environmental change, overfishing, and contamination, the requirement for global co-ordinated effort and capable stewardship becomes central. The Unified Countries Show on the Law of the Ocean (UNCLOS) gives a legitimate structure to the reasonable utilization of the seas, underlining the significance of safeguarding the marine climate to help present and people in the future.

Protecting the secrets of the dark blue is indistinguishable from the more extensive objective of accomplishing marine preservation and practical administration of sea assets. Overfishing, living space obliteration, and contamination compromise the sensitive equilibrium of marine environments, endangering the very secrets we look to comprehend. Taking on science-based preservation measures, laying out marine safeguarded regions, and advancing manageable fishing rehearses are fundamental parts of saving the trustworthiness of the dark blue for people in the future.

The profound sea, with its huge and neglected breadths, has caught the human creative mind for a really long time. From old nautical fantasies to present day stories of remote ocean investigation, the secrets of the dark blue have filled a feeling of wonderment, interest, and a longing for disclosure. Safeguarding these secrets guarantees that people in the future acquire an existence where the charm of the obscure keeps on motivating logical request, mechanical development, and a significant association with the regular world.

The significance of saving the secrets of the dark blue reaches out to the domain of logical disclosure. As we keep on investigating the profundities of the sea, new species are found, novel natural cooperations are divulged, and topographical cycles are better perceived.

The remote ocean holds hints to Earth's set of experiences, the beginnings of life, and the potential for extraterrestrial tenability. Safeguarding this boondocks of logical investigation is an interest in information and a pledge to passing on a tradition of grasping the complexities of our planet.

Additionally, the secrets of the dark blue hold undiscovered possibility for biotechnological and drug headways. Remote ocean life forms have developed remarkable transformations and biochemical mixtures that might have applications in medication, industry, and innovation. Saving these secrets guarantees that people in the future have the amazing chance to open the remedial and mechanical advantages that might emerge from the profound sea's natural fortunes.

In thinking about the significance of saving the secrets of the dark blue, it is fundamental to perceive the social and profound importance that the sea holds for some networks all over the planet. Seas have been integral to the social personalities, customs, and vocations of beach front social orders over the entire course of time. Saving the secrets of the dark blue is an affirmation of the inherent worth that the sea holds for different societies, stressing the requirement for social safeguarding close by biological preservation.

The dark blue is likewise a wellspring of motivation for human expression, writing, and inventive articulation. Endless sonnets, artistic creations, and works of writing have been roused by the sea's limitlessness, its cadenced waves, and the secrets hid underneath its surface. Saving these secrets guarantees that the wellspring of imagination and motivation drawn from the dark blue keeps on enhancing human culture and creative undertakings for a long time into the future.

As we ponder the significance of protecting the secrets of the dark blue, disregarding the developing effect of human exercises on the ocean is incomprehensible. Environmental change, plastic contamination, overfishing, and remote ocean mining present huge dangers to the wellbeing of the sea and its occupants. The desperation of tending to these difficulties highlights the requirement for prompt and purposeful endeavors to relieve the effects of human activities on the dark blue.

Environmental change, driven by the collection of ozone harming substances in the climate, is prompting climbing ocean temperatures, sea fermentation, and changes in atmospheric conditions. These progressions have extensive ramifications for marine biological systems, influencing the dissemination of species, the soundness of coral reefs, and the recurrence of outrageous climate occasions. Protecting the secrets of the dark blue requires pressing and aggregate activity to address the main drivers of environmental change and alleviate its effects on the sea.

Plastic contamination has turned into an unavoidable and major problem on the planet's seas. The gathering of plastic trash, from microplastics to enormous drifting islands, represents a danger to marine life through ingestion, snare, and territory corruption. Saving the secrets of the dark blue requires a worldwide obligation to diminishing plastic waste, further developing waste administration practices, and creating feasible choices to single-use plastics.

Overfishing, driven by unreasonable fishing rehearses and the interest for fish, exhausts fish stocks, upsets marine biological systems, and compromises the occupations of waterfront networks. Taking on feasible fishing works on, executing powerful fisheries the executives, and laying out marine safeguarded regions are fundamental stages in protecting the secrets of the dark blue and guaranteeing the drawn out soundness of sea environments.

Remote ocean mining, driven by the interest for minerals and metals, represents another wilderness of difficulties for protecting the secrets of the dark blue. The possible natural effect of mining exercises on aqueous vents, polymetallic knobs, and other remote ocean territories raises worries about irreversible harm to delicate environments. Laying out powerful administrative systems, directing careful ecological effect appraisals, and focusing on preservation endeavors are basic parts of mindful remote ocean mining rehearses.

Protecting the secrets of the dark blue requires a change in perspective by they way we view and connect with the sea. It requires a progress toward additional feasible and capable practices that focus on the soundness of marine biological systems, regard the freedoms of beach front networks, and perceive the natural worth of the sea past its monetary utility. Training, mindfulness, and support are fundamental in cultivating a shared perspective that esteems the protection of the dark blue for current and people in the future.

Pondering the significance of saving the secrets of the dark blue for people in the future prompts a significant thought of the sea's essential job in molding the World's environment, supporting different biological systems, and rousing human investigation. As we explore a time set apart by fast mechanical headway and expanding human exercises in the profound sea, it becomes basic to ponder the drawn out results of our activities and the moral obligation we bear to defend the secrets covered underneath the waves.

The dark blue, meaningful of the sweeping seas covering most of our planet, assumes a focal part in managing worldwide environment elements. Seas act as Earth's essential intensity supply, engrossing and reallocating sun based energy. The unpredictable dance of sea flows, impacted by wind examples and temperature differentials, significantly influences weather conditions and adds to the general solidness of the planet's environment. Perceiving the interconnectedness of the sea and the climate highlights the direness of protecting the trustworthiness of the dark blue to support people in the future.

Moreover, the sea is an essential part of the carbon cycle, going about as a significant sink for carbon dioxide. Phytoplankton, minute marine plants, take part in photosynthesis and assimilate carbon dioxide from the air. As necessary parts of the marine food web, phytoplankton upholds whole sea environments and assumes a basic part in sequestering carbon. Safeguarding the secrets of the dark blue is inseparable from guaranteeing the strength of marine environments and their capacity to moderate environmental change by catching and putting away carbon.

The biodiversity dwelling in the profound sea is a demonstration of the versatility and flexibility of life on The planet. From the mysterious animals close aqueous vents to the tricky species occupying the deep profundities, the dark blue has a plenty of life frames that have developed to flourish in outrageous circumstances. Safeguarding these secrets isn't simply a demonstration of protection; it is a guarantee to keeping up with the unpredictable snare of life that supports the sea and, thus, upholds earthbound life.

The moral basic to save the secrets of the dark blue emerges from the comprehension that the sea is a common worldwide asset. Notwithstanding difficulties, for example, environmental change, overfishing, and contamination, the requirement for global joint effort and mindful stewardship becomes central. The Unified Countries Show on the Law of the Ocean (UNCLOS) gives a legitimate structure to the practical utilization of the seas, underscoring the significance of safeguarding the marine climate to help present and people in the future.

Saving the secrets of the dark blue is innately attached to the more extensive objective of accomplishing marine protection and maintainable administration of sea assets. Overfishing, territory obliteration, and contamination present huge dangers to the sensitive equilibrium of marine biological systems, endangering the very secrets we try to comprehend. Taking on science-based preservation measures, laying out marine safeguarded regions, and advancing manageable fishing rehearses are fundamental parts of protecting the honesty of the dark blue for people in the future.

The profound sea, with its unfamiliar spans, has enthralled the human creative mind for a really long time. From old nautical legends to current stories of remote ocean investigation, the secrets of the dark blue have filled a feeling of wonder, interest, and a longing for revelation. Safeguarding these secrets guarantees that people in the future acquire a reality where the charm of the obscure keeps on motivating logical request, mechanical development, and a significant association with the normal world.

The significance of protecting the secrets of the dark blue stretches out to the domain of logical disclosure. As investigation of the sea's profundities proceeds, new species are found, biological communications are uncovered, and topographical cycles are better perceived. The remote ocean holds hints to Earth's set of experiences, the beginnings of life, and the potential for extraterrestrial livability. Protecting this outskirts of logical investigation is an interest in information and a pledge to passing on a tradition of figuring out the complexities of our planet.

In addition, the secrets of the dark blue proposition undiscovered possibility for biotechnological and drug progressions. Remote ocean living beings have developed novel variations and biochemical mixtures that might have applications in medication, industry, and innovation. Progressing research attempts look to distinguish and portray these significant mixtures, opening the remedial and innovative advantages that might emerge from the profound sea's natural fortunes. Saving these secrets guarantees that people in the future have the valuable chance to outfit the biotechnological and drug expected innate in the dark blue.

In pondering the significance of saving the secrets of the dark blue, it is fundamental to perceive the social and profound importance that the sea holds for some networks around the world. Seas have been integral to the social characters, customs, and occupations of beach front social orders from the beginning of time. Protecting the secrets of the dark blue is an affirmation of the inherent worth that the sea holds for different societies, underlining the requirement for social safeguarding close by biological preservation.

The dark blue likewise fills in as a wellspring of motivation for artistic expression, writing, and imaginative articulation. Endless sonnets, compositions, and works of writing have drawn motivation from the sea's limitlessness, cadenced waves, and the secrets hid underneath its surface. Safeguarding these secrets guarantees that the wellspring of inventiveness and motivation got from the dark blue keeps on advancing human culture and creative undertakings for a long time into the future.

As we ponder the significance of protecting the secrets of the dark blue, it becomes difficult to disregard the raising effect of human exercises on the sea. Environmental change, plastic contamination, overfishing, and remote ocean mining present huge dangers to the strength of the sea and its occupants. The desperation of tending to these difficulties highlights the requirement for quick and purposeful endeavors to relieve the effects of human activities on the dark blue.

Environmental change, energized by the amassing of ozone harming substances in the air, brings about climbing ocean temperatures, sea fermentation, and adjustments in weather conditions. These progressions have broad ramifications for marine biological systems, influencing species dispersion, coral reef wellbeing, and the recurrence of outrageous climate occasions. Saving the secrets of the dark blue requires critical and aggregate activity to address the main drivers of environmental change and alleviate its effects on the sea.

Plastic contamination has turned into a ubiquitous and earnest issue on the planet's seas. The development of plastic flotsam and jetsam, going from microplastics to sizable drifting islands, represents an extreme danger to marine life through ingestion, trap, and natural surroundings debasement.

Protecting the secrets of the dark blue requires a worldwide obligation to decreasing plastic waste, further developing waste administration practices, and creating maintainable choices to single-use plastics.

Overfishing, driven by impractical practices and the worldwide interest for fish, drains fish stocks, upsets marine environments, and imperils the livelihoods of waterfront networks. Embracing reasonable fishing works on, carrying out compelling fisheries the board, and laying out marine safeguarded regions are essential moves toward saving the secrets of the dark blue and guaranteeing the drawn out wellbeing of sea biological systems.

Remote ocean mining, filled by the mission for minerals and metals, presents another boondocks of difficulties for saving the secrets of the dark blue. The likely ecological effect of mining exercises on aqueous vents, polymetallic knobs, and other remote ocean living spaces raises worries about irreversible harm to delicate environments. Laying out vigorous administrative structures, directing exhaustive natural effect appraisals, and focusing on protection endeavors are basic parts of capable remote ocean mining rehearses.

Protecting the secrets of the dark blue requires a central change by they way we see and communicate with the sea. It requires a progress toward additional reasonable and mindful practices that focus on the soundness of marine biological systems, regard the freedoms of beach front networks, and perceive the inherent worth of the sea past its financial utility. Training, mindfulness, and support are fundamental in encouraging a shared mindset that esteems the protection of the dark blue for current and people in the future.

Taking everything into account, thinking about the significance of saving the secrets of the dark blue for people in the future uncovers the interconnectedness of biological, social, logical, and moral contemplations. The secrets hid underneath the sea's surface are not just logical conundrums but rather vital parts of the World's frameworks, adding to environment guideline, supporting biodiversity, and motivating human imagination. Protecting these secrets is a promise to dependable stewardship, recognizing the common obligation of shielding the sea for the prosperity of present and people in the future.

9

Conclusion

All in all, the thought of the secrets of the dark blue divulges a story that rises above logical investigation alone. An investigation of the multifaceted woven artwork ties biological versatility, social legacy, logical interest, and moral obligation. The profound sea, with its tremendous scopes and cryptic profundities, entices humankind to explore with adoration, perceiving that the protection of its secrets is crucial to the prosperity of our planet and the heritage we grant to people in the future.

The significant significance of the dark blue lies in its job as a key part in Earth's environment guideline. As the essential intensity supply, seas impact worldwide atmospheric conditions and keep up with environment soundness. Safeguarding the secrets disguised underneath the waves is inseparable from guaranteeing the proceeded with versatility of marine environments that, thusly, add to moderating environmental change. The interconnectedness of the sea and the environment highlights the criticalness of defending the dark blue as a fundamental part of Earth's life emotionally supportive network.

Biodiversity in the profound sea, adjusted to outrageous circumstances, addresses a living demonstration of the surprising flexibility of life on The planet. From the exceptional animals close aqueous vents to the slippery species in the deep profundities, the secrets of the dark blue manifest as a festival of life's variety. The demonstration of protection isn't simply a natural undertaking yet a pledge to maintaining the sensitive equilibrium of marine environments, cultivating biological versatility, and guaranteeing the coherence of life's mind boggling dance underneath the waves.

Morally, the protection of the secrets of the dark blue is a common obligation that rises above public lines. The Unified Countries Show on the Law of the Ocean (UNCLOS) gives a legitimate structure, underscoring the worldwide meaning of marine protection. Recognizing the interconnected idea of the sea forces mankind to embrace global cooperation and capable stewardship. Safeguarding the dark blue turns into a moral goal, cherishing the idea that the sea isn't simply an asset to take advantage of yet a common heritage to safeguard to help present and people in the future.

The objective of marine protection and feasible sea the executives becomes fundamental chasing saving the secrets of the dark blue. Overfishing, territory annihilation, and contamination undermine the sensitive harmony of marine biological systems. Sticking to science-based preservation measures, laying out marine safeguarded regions, and advancing reasonable fishing rehearses are crucial stages. These endeavors guarantee the life span of the secrets we look to disentangle, encouraging a harmony between human exercises and the conservation of the dark blue for a long time into the future.

Past the unmistakable biological and moral aspects, the dark blue holds social and otherworldly importance for networks all over the planet. Beach front social orders have woven the sea into their social personalities, customs, and jobs. Safeguarding the secrets of the dark blue is an affirmation of the inborn worth that the sea holds for assorted societies. It means a pledge to safeguarding the natural uprightness of the sea as well as the social legacy implanted in its waves, flows, and profundities.

The dark blue fills in as a wellspring of motivation for human expression, writing, and imaginative articulation. Craftsmen, artists, and essayists have drawn motivation from its immeasurability, cadenced waves, and the secrets hid underneath its surface. Protecting these secrets guarantees that the wellspring of innovativeness and motivation got from the dark blue keeps on advancing human culture and imaginative undertakings for a long time into the future. It turns into an interest in the immaterial yet significant association among mankind and the sea, encouraging a getting through relationship with the secrets that dazzle the human soul.

Deductively, the secrets of the dark blue address a wilderness of investigation that stretches out past the known limits of our planet. The journey for grasping Earth's set of experiences, the starting points of life, and the potential for extraterrestrial tenability is complicatedly connected to remote ocean investigation. Saving this logical boondocks is an interest in information, offering experiences into planetary cycles and the development of life on The planet. It holds the commitment of disentangling the secrets of our own planet as well as giving significant illustrations to figuring out the possible tenability of other divine bodies.

Biotechnological and drug headways further highlight the expected intrinsic in the secrets of the dark blue. Remote ocean creatures, with their novel transformations and biochemical mixtures, offer a mother lode of opportunities for medication, industry, and innovation. Saving these secrets guarantees that people in the future have the chance to open the helpful and mechanical advantages that might emerge from the profound sea's organic fortunes. It addresses a pledge to manageable bioprospecting and dependable usage of the dark blue's biotechnological potential.

In any case, as we examine the meaning of safeguarding the secrets of the dark blue, it is difficult to overlook the mounting difficulties presented by human exercises. Environmental change, plastic contamination, overfishing, and remote ocean mining cast a shadow over the sea's wellbeing and essentialness. Dire and deliberate endeavors are expected to address the main drivers of these difficulties and moderate their effects. Safeguarding the secrets of the dark blue requires an extraordinary change in our relationship with the sea, encouraging mankind to take on additional feasible practices and cultivate an amicable concurrence with this huge and complex environment.

In confronting these difficulties, the source of inspiration turns out to be clear - a call for aggregate liability, informed direction, and a pledge to supportable practices. Whether through worldwide cooperation, severe administrative structures, or individual way of life decisions, each commitment assumes a part in the protection of the secrets of the dark blue. The desperation is highlighted by the irreversible idea of specific ecological effects, accentuating the requirement for quick and significant change.

Safeguarding the secrets of the dark blue isn't simply an obligation; it is an interest from now on - a future where the sea keeps on moving, support, and support life in the entirety of its structures. It is a dream of an existence where the dark blue remaining parts a wellspring of marvel and revelation, where the obscure keeps on coaxing researchers, pioneers, and visionaries the same. The secrets disguised underneath the waves hold the way to opening the privileged insights of our planet, our starting points, and the more extensive universe.

Generally, the secrets of the dark blue rise above the limits of logical disciplines, social settings, and moral contemplations. They address a common legacy, a wellspring of motivation, and a supply of information that rises above ages. Safeguarding these secrets is an affirmation of our interconnectedness with the sea and a promise to granting a heritage that guarantees the dark blue keeps on charming, support, and rouse the interest of mankind for a long time into the future. The source of inspiration resonates as an aggregate undertaking to safeguard and protect the secrets of the dark blue - an immortal and all inclusive heritage that has a place with every one of us.

www.ingramcontent.com/pod-product-compliance
Lightning Source LLC
LaVergne TN
LVHW021238080526
838199LV00088B/4571